WITHDRAWN FROM
DEVON LIBRARY SERVICES

Steam Railways in Industry

1 Steam scuds and scatters as Stewarts & Lloyds Minerals 57 heads homeward from Harringworth

2 S 111 *Airedale No.* 2 waits in the September sun whilst spoil is discharged at Savile Colliery.

Steam Railways in Industry

Colin T Gifford and Horace Gamble

B T Batsford Limited
London

Dedication

To Eric Tonks who engineered the alliance which pioneered this book.

First published 1976
Text © Horace Gamble 1976
Photographs © Colin T Gifford 1976
All rights are reserved. No part of
this publication may be reproduced,
in any form or by any means, without
permission from the publishers
Filmset by
Servis Filmsetting Ltd, Manchester
Printed in Great Britain by
The Anchor Press, Tiptree, Essex
for the publishers B T Batsford Ltd
4 Fitzhardinge Street, London W1H 0AH

ISBN 0 7134 3155 5

Acknowledgments

An endeavour has been made by both word and picture, within the compass of a single volume, to portray a reasonably wide selection of industrial locomotive types and the environment in which they served during the twilight years of steam. Not unnaturally this has meant leaning rather heavily on a variety of sources for the acquisition and checking of facts and figures, for reading the drafts and in making useful suggestions. One doubts whether the perfect book has yet been written, despite every care which may be taken, and so any errors found within the text must be laid firmly at my door.

Where no scrapping date is given it may be assumed that the locomotive described was still in existence at the beginning of 1975. Preserved locomotives have lately acquired a disquieting habit of moving around and present locations may differ from those known at the time of writing.

Grateful thanks are therefore given in respect of willing assistance to the following members of the Industrial Railway Society: L. G. Charlton; C. Craven; A. R. Etherington; S. A. Leleux; T. J. Lodge; J. W. Lowe; C. E. Mountford; K. P. Plant; E. S. Tonks; R. E. West; D. N. Wignall; M. Wignall; and W. K. Williams; also to Messrs. H. D. Bowtell (Industrial Locomotive Society); V. J. Bradley (Llanberis Lake Railway); J. F. Clay; S. Lowery (Seaham Harbour Dock Co.); R. L. Ratcliffe (Sittingbourne & Kemsley Light Railway) and B. D. Stoyel. The verse is reproduced by kind permission of the Editor 'Industrial Railway Record'. My wife has shown enthusiastic encouragement throughout accompanied by a never failing supply of coffee, and finally I would like to express my appreciation to Colin Gifford for placing his confidence in me to provide the commentary.

I hope that this matches up to his magnificent photographs.

H. A. Gamble
Leicester 1975

Contents

Dedication and Acknowledgments
page 4

Preface
page 6

Grass Roots
page 9

Down to the Sea in Trucks – Seaham Harbour
page 17

From Ironstone to Steel – Corby
page 26

Steam under the City
page 40

King Coal the First
page 48

King Coal the Second
page 72

Kentish Paper – Sittingbourne
page 80

Snowdonia Slate
page 87

Appreciation
page 92

Steam in Twilight
page 95

Index
page 96

Preface

Railway enthusiasts seem to have acquired through the media a somewhat dubious image; they are represented as being slightly kinky individuals who spend precious time and money on collecting useless trivia in the shape of station, trackside and rolling stock relics, for no better purpose than trying to resurrect a bygone and increasingly dim past. If not that, then they are accused of merely playing trains along decrepit branch lines, with antediluvian vehicles towed by superannuated Puffing Billies.

In truth the hobby embraces a wide panoply of sub-divisions, ranging over such aspects as social history, politics, architecture, engineering, mechanics, signalling, to mention but a few. But above all, that supreme creation, the steam locomotive commands fanatical idolatry. Why? Those who fall under its spell and become addicted to its every facet will vow that it is the nearest thing to a living being; that it has heart and soul and voice, and combines personality with symmetrically curvacious good looks. It is rumoured that in certain quarters there are those who find other forms of motive power attractive. For that matter some still believe that the earth is flat; or that Hitler is still alive. *Dulce est dispere in loco!* Whatever one's particular bent, there should be no gainsaying the thesis that the railway scene is mentally stimulating to anyone who has successfully survived the train-spotting phase. Then it becomes not so much a hobby, but more a way of life in which a camera should be deemed the most indispensable aid.

Railway photography has been practised for a hundred and twenty years or more, yet it is only in the past few decades that it has emerged with a new concept and significance. Even now the majority of shutter-clicking enthusiasts are prone to expend too much film on purely 'record' shots, which rightly claim their place in history, but have not the breadth of vision which creates a work of art.

During the years up to the middle 'thirties the typical railway photograph was a three-quarter front view of a train in open country, or alternatively, at a platform, with the back sun shining straight along the parting on the photographer's head. Many were technically brilliant, of course, and all credit is due to the cameramen in 'stopping' for all time those long departed, magnificent locomotives, with their majestic trains. Just when a fresh dimension was emerging, in which lineside furniture was used to add interest rather than detract from the main subject, the outbreak of war brought an understandable ban on this aspect of the hobby. Nevertheless the seeds had been sown for a different angle on railway photography, in which pictorial composition was to play as great a role as the subject and in which pictures were not merely records but mentally as well as visually stimulating. We had for too long been strangled by convention or afraid to attempt the seemingly impossible.

But beauty being 'in the eye of the beholder' it is a very subjective thing. It was therefore with much controversy that an *avant-garde* mode of photography was greeted in the railway periodicals just over a decade ago, and quickly dubbed 'the new approach'. Why anyone should have taken exception to it is not easily understood for much of it presented railway scenes exactly as the enthusiast saw them through his own eyes but had never before had the courage to portray them. Highly acknowledged among those who did, is Colin Gifford.

Not all photographers had the imaginative originality to see the rich scope for pictorial composition presented by such scenes as muddy tramways wending their way between slag tips, but industrial railways lend themselves to exciting camera work by their very diversity of location. There is a strange and fascinating beauty in gasworks, pit-head gear, steel retorts and shipyard cranes (unless you happen to live next door) and to the imaginative photographer such backcloths are ideal foils for the fussing little locomotives shepherding truck loads of raw materials in all the diverse industries in which they played so crucial a role. At the other extreme, for those who prefer something more pretty, there were the ironstone railways (sadly moribund and now quite steamless) threading their rural ways through cool green countryside where the sight of an industrial train appeared incongruous. In more productive, and steamier days, such quarry lines were a joy to behold and many of us would be in a dilemma to say from which we derived the greater satisfaction – the sight of the struggle of a diminutive saddle-tank engine lifting four ore-laden waggons up a boulder strewn gully, or the effortless flight of a main line Pacific-hauled fifteen coach express. The focal point in both scenes was the steam loco, each within its own context equally thrilling.

The steam locomotive was originally employed solely in industry and many would claim was the invention which, above all others, was to enhance the prosperity of the nation. The wheel has turned full circle; for the remaining steam engines regularly working in this country – barring of course preservation and pleasure lines – are to be found in their original environment. In view of this, it does appear strange that their recorded history is so scant compared with that of main line railways, but this is probably because the latter have always been more familiar to the public. Industrial lines were more secluded, usually operating in less salubrious surroundings. Yet they were not all hidden from the public eye, for instance it is not so long ago that contractors ceased to use railways as the means of transport in construction work and on building sites. One contractor alone employed about two hundred locomotives on the building of the Manchester Ship Canal. Nor were the tramways of the various minerals' quarries confined to the fields, skirting and crossing country roads as was their wont. In Burton-on-Trent, the populace might have been forgiven any disenchantment with the humble, but gorgeous orange, or blue, brass adorned beer engines which were forever levelcrossing practically every street. The town could have been likened to an enormous marshalling yard with the houses, shops, offices and factories neatly fitted into the spaces between the twenty two miles of tracks over whose routes now trundle rubber-soled Leyland lorries.

Industrial railway enthusiasts are not an entirely new breed though their number seems to have grown during the decline of steam on the main lines due to the modernization programme. Photography of industrial railways *per se*, rather than their locomotives alone, is however a more recent innovation, but one should not forget the early pioneers such as George Alliez, Frank Jones and Derek Stoyel, without whose photographic records much knowledge of the subject would have been lost without trace. The pity is that there were not men of their genre around in the last century. It is encouraging to realize that there are dedicated groups of people, like the Industrial Railway Society, who through persisted efforts are, even now, discovering hitherto unknown sites where private railways were located. Even so there may be scores of locations and hundreds of locomotives (for there were over two hundred locomotive builders in this country alone) which will never be traced. Just how long the steam locomotive will continue to be used is highly speculative for, of the remaining lines which have not turned, or are turning, to diesel traction, many are constantly being closed in favour of road vehicles. There are various factors to be considered, all of which weigh heavily against steam although a number of relatively modern locomotives remain, which by previous standards should be good for many decades; the difficulty in obtaining spare parts militates against them. It is not unknown for locomotives to be out of traffic for almost two years on this account and in terms of hard cash this is not a paying proposition. However, steam locomotives are still being overhauled, and though many are retained merely as an occasional stand-in, one might hope to see them, if seldom, for a few more years.

There is little point, at this late stage of the game, in evangelizing; though it may encourage a quest for further knowledge of the past and a more enlightened interest in industrial locomotives operating on preserved railways. Nor is it prudent to preach to the converted, but rather let them savour the pictures and indulge in what is fondly known as nostalgia. As for those for whom the railways hold a certain tenuous fascination, but who are not owned, body and soul, by them, one hopes that they will discover not only what makes enthusiasts enthuse but how the inspiration of Colin Gifford has captured the spirit of the railways and made poetry in pictures with the camera.

This then, is first and foremost a picture gallery employing a guide to show you around, and in passing offer a comment or two which may help to heighten your pleasure in what you are viewing. The opinions expressed are entirely personal, and if Gifford is not depending on a banker, then he is certainly taking on a gamble!

3 Robert Stephenson's Works No. 1 of 1825, *Locomotion* at Bank Top station Darlington where it has watched trains come and go since 1890.

4 A Coalbrookdale product of *c.*1865 returned home to retirement in 1959.

5 Two gauges at Blaenau Ffestiniog. The 1 ft 11½ in. of the Festiniog crosses swords with the GWR 4 ft 8½ in. near Duffws.

6 Howgill Waggon Brake at Whitehaven Harbour. An inclined plane at approximately the same location was in operation in the first half of the eighteenth century.

Grass Roots

Experiments in harnessing steam for the provision of power first blossomed into practical fruition with the Newcomen designed pumping engines (later improved upon by Watt) early in the eighteenth century, and by 1712 these were sufficiently advanced to be put into service in industry. One hundred years later the first reliable travelling steam engines were at work, but even these had been preceded some two centuries by industrial railways. Waggonways, tramroads, or rayle-ways were known in this country at the beginning of the seventeenth century: the earliest authenticated example being that from Wollaton Lane End to Strelley in Nottinghamshire – a distance of two miles. Constructed of wood, about 1603–4, its purpose was to facilitate an easier passage for coal-laden waggons than was possible on the deeply rutted roads. This, the first British historically recorded 'industrial railway', though short and rudimentary in construction, was the precursor of many similar horse-drawn tramways, of which at least one thousand five hundred miles are known to have existed. The advent and general adoption of the steam locomotive did not preclude their continued construction up to the 1860s, and the use of equestrian motive power continued, albeit to a diminishing extent, for another hundred years.

Confusion and controversy has sometimes arisen over the usage of the words 'tramway' and 'railway' probably owing to the universal use of the former for passenger carrying tramcars along public highways. Fundamentally, they are one and the same thing because both words are derived from the same source, the difference lying in the country of origin. From Scandinavia came the word *tromm* meaning log; from Germany *traam*: a beam; and from France *reille*: a rail, the latter being the horizontal wood bar in gates and fences. Waggons which carried skips of coal along the roads were constructed of a wooden frame of 'traams' from which the term tram arose, and was applied to such vehicles as early as the sixteenth century. The essential structure of a waggonway was two parallel lengths of rectangular timber ('rails') spiked to cross-bearers (the sleepers) which were set into the ground; essentially like a railway, in the now accepted sense, though then built with different materials.

The earliest rails, fashioned from English hardwoods, were greater in width than in height, to be substantial enough to carry the waggons with their flanged wooden wheels. Ballast was spread over the sleepers to provide a road surface on which the horses could find sure footing. From the Midlands (another waggonway built 1605 was from a colliery at Calcotts to the river Severn at Brosely in Salop) the system spread to Northumberland and Durham, where a large proportion of the coal mined was carried by waggonway to the rivers Tyne and Wear for shipment by sea to London or abroad. By the end of the seventeenth century, waggonways were appearing in the coal and iron areas of South Wales: the first was in all probability at the Melwyn Works near Neath. By 1722 Scotland had one from Tranent Coal Pits to Cockenzie Old Harbour on the Forth. Such was the intensive use of the new form of transportation that repair and replacement of the wooden rails became necessary with increasing frequency; equally, the waggon wheels also suffered from similar wear and tear. Something more durable was required, but evidently the apparently logical step of applying iron to both wheels and rails was accomplished only in two separate stages. In 1731 iron was found to be used for tyres and spokes of waggons in Sunderland, but not until some seven years later is it known that cast iron strips were applied to the tops of the wooden rails. All was not well even then, for the plates had a disconcerting habit of detaching themselves from the rails. The original concept of one horse to one waggon was now giving way to increased loads, causing detrimental effects upon the track. Bearing in mind the fact that by the middle of the century there were up to fifty colliery waggonways in the north-east, some as much as ten miles long, and that every ironworks in South Wales had its lines for the conveyance of ironstone, limestone and coal, the problem of track maintenance under such circumstances must have proved something of a bugbear.

With the industrial revolution gaining momentum, there was a great resurgence in the iron-making industry, particularly in Shropshire where at Coalbrookdale – famed for its iron bridges and cast-iron cylinders for steam engines – iron rails of rectangular section were first cast and laid down in 1767. Other railways adopted them shortly afterwards in the Midlands and on Tyneside, but it was not until late in the century that they were to be used in Wales. Certainly they were not manufactured much before 1790 at Penydarren iron works, in Glamorgan, where a momentous experiment was to be carried out fourteen years later. Transition from wood to iron (and from iron to steel) was not, however, a straightforward progress, for there was a period when several systems co-existed one of which transferred the flanges from wheels to rails. This pattern, known as tramplates, or plateways, became common in South Wales around 1794, though it had been used in Sheffield nearly twenty years previously. The rails were of L-section, spiked down to wooden sleepers, or stone blocks from 1802, for the use of flangeless wheels and it was on such a plateway that Trevithick's locomotive ran at Penydarren in 1804. Benjamin Outram of Butterley Ironworks was a keen protagonist of this form of railway but although it found favour in the south and in Scotland it was little employed in the north-east coalfield, one notable exception being at Wylam Colliery. For some twenty-five years this method was employed in new constructions, and in the conversion of waggonways in certain localities, but with the introduction of the steam locomotive a gradual process of conversion to edge-rails began to take place in the 1840s. Immediately prior to this was the introduction of a dual system whereby the vertical flange of the L-section rail was widened to give a running surface to flangeless wheels; at the same time the horizontal web could still accommodate wheels without flanges. This ingenious idea did not have a very long reign for the weaknesses inherent in cast-iron rails, when subjected to the heavier weight and thrust of locomotives, were still apparent in the high incidence of breakages.

Edge-rails had taken many shapes and forms – rectangular, inverted-L, and even oval – but the forerunner of the once universal I-section, or bull-head rail, was the T-section perfected in 1816 by William Losh, a Newcastle iron-founder. George Stephenson, celebrated for his persistence in improving and promoting the steam locomotive, applied his imagination in other directions also, and the emergence of the chair and rail manufactured by Losh are accredited to him. A further important step in the evolution of trackwork more suited to the new form of locomotion was the adoption of malleable, or wrought, iron for rails. Such rails had been used successfully in 1808 and were probably originally introduced just after the turn of the century, but were a product of Bedlington iron works from 1820 onwards. Stephenson saw the great potential offered by the superior strength of wrought-iron which allowed rails of greater length to be employed with safety, and, despite his financial interest in the Losh patent, convinced the directors of the projected railway from Stockton to Darlington that it was in their best interest to use malleable rails at least for the main line.

It was in 1856 that Henry Bessemer's process made possible a reduction in the cost of steel production; nevertheless malleable iron was still a comparatively cheaper commodity which, for reasons of economy, the railways were loath to abandon. The Midland Railway was the first to experiment with steel rails – at Derby station in 1857 – but this was an isolated case, and after sixteen years of wear and tear they were removed. However, it was the London & North Western and the North Eastern railways who, in 1862, took the bolder step of laying steel rails at busy junctions, and by the end of the decade this material was generally adopted by the major companies. Weights and lengths of rail gradually increased over the years; welded rail was introduced, and finally the flat-bottomed spiked rail of continental antecedence became standard on passenger main lines in the post-nationalization years. Although industrial systems never had occasion to use welded rail, flat-bottom track was common long before British Railways adopted its use. Narrow gauge lines were almost exclusively laid with rail of like section. Narrow gauge is defined as a railway of less than 4 ft 8½ in. between the inner surfaces of the running rails, which begs the question as to why this rather abstruse dimension evolved as the standard railway gauge. In the days of horse-drawn, or even hand-propelled, waggonways the gauge was suited to the particular width of the vehicles running upon it and each individual owner laid tracks to suit his own requirements, but even so a broad pattern was to emerge. Thus, 4 ft 0 in. and upwards was favoured in the northern regions, 3 ft 0 in. and over was common in South Wales, while the west Midlands went in for narrower gauges of 1 ft 8 in. to 2 ft 4½ in. The quarry railways of North Wales were around the 2 ft 0 in. mark: an optimum gauge for formerly manually operated lines. Outram, of tramplate fame, settled on 4 ft 2 in. for the majority of his railways in the Midlands and even envisaged a national network on this gauge. Because of his predilection for plate rails it has been claimed, more than once, that 'tramroads' was a contraction of 'Outram-roads', but in actual fact the word was in common use a century or so before Outram was born. George Stephenson's first locomotives, at Killingworth, were built to a gauge of 4 ft 8 in. to suit the existing waggonway, which he adopted for the later Hetton Colliery line and for the Stockton & Darlington Railroad. Robert Stephenson, George's son, engineered his railways to 4 ft $8\frac{1}{2}$ in. gauge. The additional half inch may have been added as an easement for freer running, or to allow for variations in the manufacture of rolling stock. It may be claimed that the Stephenson family fortuitously created the standard gauge by the mere expedient of standardizing locomotive production to that decreed by the width of the original track at Killingworth.

In the main, the private railways serving factories, docks, pits and quarries were laid to the standard gauge so as to facilitate the interchange of waggons with the main lines, but there was also a large proportion of narrow gauge railways in industry which, on account of their relative portability and smaller capital outlay, were very popular where transfer of goods could be effected to other forms of transport, be it rail, road or water. There were many solely narrow gauge lines for the conveyance of materials between processing plants on the same premises, and there were other locations where at least two different gauges were laid down in addition to standard gauge. Another method was in the use of transporter waggons, whereby the narrow gauge rolling stock could be carried pick-a-back fashion on a wider gauge, though not necessarily standard. An excellent example of this was the Padarn Railway of 4 ft 0 in. gauge, in Caernarvonshire, which carried the 1 ft $10\frac{3}{4}$ in. gauge slate waggons from Llanberis to Port Dinorwic on the Menai Straits. Very few broad gauge systems in industry are recorded. One, of five miles length, was used between quarries and Holyhead breakwater and one of its 7 ft $0\frac{1}{4}$ in. gauge locomotives may still be at work in the Azores! Probably the widest ever was one of 10 ft 11 in. at Colvilles Ironworks, Motherwell. The locomotives presented a most crab-like appearance.

Regular passenger carrying by rail was first introduced by the horsedrawn Swansea & Mumbles Railway in 1807, some two centuries after the early industrial systems came into being. The scene is now set for the introduction of the steam travelling engine into industry (and indeed the world) for its use as passenger motive power was not to come until a little later.

Richard Trevithick, a Cornishman well versed in the skills of stationary steam engine building and development, made the first use of steam to motivate carriages on public roads, with some success, and it was he who conceived the idea of applying the same principle to travelling tramroad engines. His early experiments were carried out at Coalbrookdale in 1802, where an engine was built under his supervision to demonstrate the power of high pressure steam. The Coalbrookdale company was duly impressed and undertook to build an engine for the railway, which had been laid down in 1767, employing Trevithick as its designer, but although he possessed the necessary foresight and ingenuity, he was lacking in perseverance, succumbing easily to hostility towards his bold notions. Steam engines, it was said, were all right in their place, which was not upon the roads or tramways. George Stephenson came up against this same opposition but his fanatical faith led to eventual triumph. Trevithick, having business elsewhere, left Coalbrookdale to its own devices and there is no evidence to say whether the first railway locomotive was ever completed. The following year saw Trevithick at the Penydarren Ironworks in Merthyr Tydfil erecting a forge engine, which was followed by the building of a steam tram engine. It was intended to haul 10-ton loads of bar iron along the nine mile 4 ft 2 in. plateway to Navigation House, Abercynon, on the Glamorganshire Canal. When completed, in 1804, it was put to work between the furnaces and the old forge, but despite the fact that it worked very well its weight played havoc with the track. One apocryphal account states that after encouraging trials the locomotive made one uncompleted journey along the 'main line'. With a 25-ton load on gradients as severe as 1 in 36, and with numerous sharp curves, the locomotive broke so many tramplates that it was ignominiously hauled back by horses and thereafter used as a stationary engine. According to Trevithick, several return journeys were made but its career as a tramway locomotive lasted, it seems, less than two months.

The third locomotive designed by Trevithick was built in 1805 at Gateshead, for the Wylam Colliery, but after being tested there it was not accepted by the management and this too became a stationary engine. Trevithick died penniless and unlauded in 1833, but he had laid down several important principles, some of which were not readily appreciated by his contemporaries and successors. He had established that a smooth iron wheel would run on an iron rail by adhesion alone, and by the use of discharging the waste steam into the chimney had created the steamblast whereby the fire was more forcefully drawn, giving better steaming qualities to the boiler.

John Blenkinsop, the owner of the Middleton

Colliery railway, Leeds, which had been built in 1758 as a 4 ft 1 in. gauge wooden tramway, became interested in the 'Iron Horse', but was of the opinion that adhesion would not be sufficient to enable a locomotive to draw 100 tons, as desired. Consequently, in 1811 he patented a rack and pinion device, which was fitted to the first of four similar locomotives built by Fenton, Murray & Wood of Leeds. Connecting rods from the cylinders (of which there were two as opposed to Trevithick's one) drove a cog wheel which engaged in a toothed rack rail, laid outside the running rails, by now relaid with iron to 5 ft 0 in. gauge. The 5-ton locomotive was put to work in 1812, hauling coal on the three and a half mile line to canal staithes, and on level track it moved a train of 94 tons. The four locomotives continued to work the traffic until 1835, but after their demise were not replaced and the owners reverted to horse traction for another thirty years. Although they had done what was required of them, and, having two cylinders with opposed cranks, were an advance on the Penydarren locomotive, Matthew Murray had employed a single flue which reduced the steaming rate of the boiler. Trevithick's locomotives were built with a return fire tube, a practice taken up by Hedley and Hackworth, but not by George Stephenson, who relied on a wide diameter flue to increase the heating surface.

In the year following the introduction of steam locomotion at Middleton, Blenkinsop rack-type engines were in use on the five mile, 4 ft $7\frac{1}{2}$ in. gauge, Kenton & Coxlodge Railway at Wallsend, and on a two mile line of 4 ft 0 in. gauge at Orrell Colliery near Wigan. At the same time William Hedley, an overseer at Wylam Colliery, convinced that rack propulsion was unnecessary, conducted a series of experiments on what amounted to a locomotive under-frame loaded with iron, the conclusions from which were that adhesion alone would enable a travelling engine to work successfully on the track. Hedley employed Thomas Waters, an engineer of Gateshead, to assist in the construction of his first locomotive, reverting to a single cylinder and one fire tube. As might have been expected, it frequently ran out of steam, but Hedley set about remedying the defects by designing a second locomotive embodying Trevithick's features of return flue with a blast pipe, though it was, by all accounts, a rebuild of the first. Having largely overcome the problem of 'shy' steaming, there was still the matter of weight. Tramplates were still a very expendable commodity, so much so that spare lengths were carried on the locomotive to effect immediate repairs as the plates became broken. In an effort to alleviate this nuisance, attempts were made to spread the weight by carrying the machine on eight wheels. The unevenness of the track, however, caused the rigid engine frame to lift wheels clear of the plates, thus putting all the weight on the remaining axles, and resulting only in *status quo*! Nevertheless, two of the three Hedley locomotives (*Wylam Dilly, Puffing Billy* and *Lady Mary*) worked the 5 ft 0 in. gauge, five mile line from the colliery to the river for about fifty years, making them true contenders for the term successful.

George Stephenson, who was born at Wylam in Northumberland amid colliery surroundings and had received no formal education, had by dint of hard work now progressed to engine-wright at Killingworth Colliery where he envisaged the use of locomotives to supplant horses. His first design, named *Blucher* after a local colliery, followed the Murray tradition of having a single boiler flue, though he had studied the products of Hedley at Wylam, with the result that it was little more advantageous than horse-power on this 4 ft 8 in. edge-rail line. Stephenson's second attempt, built one year later, in 1815, once more employed a single fire tube but with the addition of two steam exhausts into the chimney, and proved to be a better steaming machine. A further progressive step was the provision of coupling rods placed on crank axles between the wheels, but unfortunately in this form they were not a success and were removed in favour of chain and sprocket couplings. To overcome the wearing effects caused by the absence of springing, Stephenson and Losh designed steam springs, acting on pistons, protruding from the underside of the boiler to each of the wheels. This patent was embodied in a Killingworth engine in 1816 and for some six years was standard in Stephenson's machines, although from *c.* 1820 steel leaf springs, in conjunction with heavier track, became normal practice.

During the years of trial, in which the new machines were being improved steadily by the colliery engineers, their exploits had become widely known and pit owners in other areas were anxious to employ the new form of transportation. A Newcastle locomotive was tried out at Whitehaven in 1816, but the flimsy track conspired to its demise; likewise the Kilmarnock & Troon Railway imported a Stephenson loco in 1819 which also proved a failure. It was now the turn of County Durham to enter the arena where, in 1822, a 4 ft 8 in. edge-rail track was laid from Hetton-le-Hole to the river Wear, a distance of eight miles, with five of Stephenson's Killingworth type locomotives to work the sections not cable hauled. These were withdrawn in 1827, which suggests that no improvement had been gained over the original design. Meanwhile, Stephenson had been appointed as surveyor to a proposed railway to carry coal from Witton Park mine to Shildon, over cable-worked inclines, and thence onward to Stockton, via Darlington, by locomotive. Together with his son, Robert, they became absorbed in the mechanical and engineering problems encountered in designing a locomotive to work on the new railway. Robert's extraordinary talent and enthusiasm towards the project – he was at the time working as an overseer at Killingworth – culminated in his father obtaining permission for him to leave the colliery for a 6-month course in chemistry at Edinburgh University. Upon his return in 1823 he rejoined his father and together they established the Engine Works in Forth Street, Newcastle. From 1824 to 1827 he was employed in supervising the erection of mining machinery in South America and on returning to England became manager of the Newcastle firm, known as Robert Stephenson & Co., which continued building locomotives under that name until the amalgamation with Messrs. Hawthorn Leslie & Co. Ltd in 1937. During his absence the Stockton & Darlington Railroad had been opened, in 1825, again to 4 ft 8 in. gauge with edge-rails, and although it had been intended as a goods railway, passenger trains were operated with horse traction, except for the opening ceremony when Stephenson's *Locomotion* (Works number 1) hauled the inaugural train – albeit with chaldron waggons – but it was not until 1833 that steam replaced horses on passenger duties, and only in 1840, was it converted to standard gauge. *Locomotion* and the other three Stephenson locomotives were slow and cumbersome and it was upon Robert that the task of designing a speedier machine fell.

A third member of the mining community at Wylam was also destined to leave his mark as an improver of the travelling engine. Timothy Hackworth served his apprenticeship in the engine house at Wylam Colliery, taking an active part in the construction of Hedley's locomotives and in 1824 was appointed by the elder Stephenson as the acting manager of the Forth Street Works during the absence overseas of his son. When Robert Stephenson took over as head of the firm, Hackworth was offered a partnership but declined, having set his ambition towards establishing a Works of his own. However, George Stephenson persuaded him to accept the post of resident engineer on the Stockton & Darlington Railroad. The locomotives had not attained the expectations of the directors who were in favour of abandoning them, but Hackworth, who was cast in the same mould as the Stephensons and saw a great future for mechanical traction, would not give way, and promised to build for them a superior machine. His persistence was rewarded, but on the stipulation that he used the boiler of an earlier locomotive, only one year old, built by Wilsons of Newcastle and having four cylinders exhausting steam into a single blast pipe. *Royal George*, as the engine was named, worked on the Stockton & Darlington until 1842, but even so the secret of producing a fast, light and reliable locomotive had not been discovered.

A Manchester to Liverpool railway was projected in 1824, first as a carrier of goods, but soon became extended in concept to provide a means of conveying passengers as well. George Stephenson was its engineer. At the outset there was controversy over the motive power and cable haulage nearly won the day until the celebrated Rainhill Trials of 1829 showed that the steam locomotive was to become the solution to future transport needs. Of the four locomotives entered into competition two were quickly eliminated, while Stephenson's *Rocket* (Works No. 19) eventually triumphed over Hackworth's *Sanspariel*, which was not only heavier and unreliable, but could not match the maximum speed of 29 m.p.h. set up by *Rocket*. Here was the first example of the multi-tube boiler, on which succeeding generations of locomotive engineers have relied; it was designed and built by Robert Stephenson from a suggestion made to his father by Mr Henry Booth of the Liverpool & Manchester Railway.

When the railway opened in 1830, the first train was drawn by *Northumbrian*, another Stephenson built locomotive, which was in essence the prototype of the conventional locomotive. Cylinders, which had hitherto been vertical or steeply inclined, were now placed horizontally alongside the fire-box (a practice soon to be discontinued in favour of cylinders under the level of the smoke-box), the fire-box was constructed with a water jacket as an integral part of the boiler, and a smoke-box appeared at the fore end for the first time.

The railway locomotive, which had originally been designed for the haulage of minerals, had become capable of handling passenger trains at speeds far in excess of stage coaches and was now entrenched, beyond all opposition. But although passenger-type engines became larger and larger as the demand for speed and passenger carrying capacity became greater, the industrial locomotive, by virtue of its unchanging role, remained to the end mainly of the same four or six wheel formation as the coal engines of Hedley, Hackworth and Stephenson. That is not to say that there were no substantial improvements. Far from it, for the 100-ton loads of the pioneers rose to 1000 tons a century and a quarter later. There was one very important difference in that the separate tender, employed for carrying fuel and water supplies, gave way to the 'tank' type locomotive in which these essential commodities were housed on

the same frame as the boiler and cylinders. This handy arrangement is said to have been introduced by the firm of William Fairbairn of Manchester about 1840. Various styles and positions of the water tanks evolved – back, pannier, saddle, side and well – the saddle being the most popular in industrial service, for it gave an uninterrupted access to the motion between the frames and could be readily lifted off when repairs became necessary. The fact that the locomotive became more top heavy than with the other types of tank was of little consequence at the slow speeds normally required of them. However, not all of the motive power used in industry was of the tank variety, as there was a small minority of tender engines to be found in Scotland and in the Northumberland–Durham coal mining areas (where else!). In passing, it is interesting to note that *Rocket* itself became an industrial locomotive in 1836, being sold to a Cumberland colliery line. This was probably the first instance of a main line locomotive being purchased for further use in industry, a practice which still obtains to this day. After withdrawal in 1840, it was later returned to the Newcastle Works until in 1862 it was bestowed to posterity at the Kensington Science Museum. Was this act the harbinger of the present preservation movement?

Thus the coal trade had given birth to rayle-ways two hundred years before the advent of the steam locomotive. This in turn was the progeny of the coal and iron concerns, a quarter of a century before its regular use outside of industry was implemented. The Industrial Revolution led to the railway mania by virtue of which it had become an explosion. That which it begat caused it to prosper umpteenfold. Since those far off days, ironstone quarrying, steel manufacturing and coal mining have continued in the forefront, with railways exclusive to their own use, many of which were (some still are) extensive, and rich in the variety of locomotive types then used. In seeking out these worthy subjects for photography, enthusiasts have, perhaps unwittingly, paid their homage to those engineers of the nineteenth century.

7 Seaham Harbour grab dredger *Wynyard* grapples with the mud while the Lewin (*c*.1870) and the maintenance train look on from the North Pier.
8 *Eppleton Hall,* with 'slow astern' on the telegraph, manoeuvres a motor vessel into the South Dock, Seaham. (August 1966)

9 Hawthorn Leslie 3898 of 1936, *Neptune*, chucks black stuff up the chimney faster than the fireman can assuage its appetite. Performance along the inebriated track on the left would make for an interesting spectacle. *Neptune* spent all its working life at Seaham until broken up in 1967.

10 173 (Hawthorn Leslie 3919 of 1937) with spillage waggons, crashes through the undergrowth and heads out to grass as if followed by the Demon Diesel. Formerly at the Acklam Works of Dorman Long 173 has white warning patches instead of the yellow more common elsewhere. These disappeared when the engine was scrapped in 1967. (August 1966)

11 A flagman guards the crossing on South Crescent while local 'gaffers' immune to the sight look the other way. 177 (R. Stephenson & Hawthorn 7036 of 1940) displays its oil tank atop the saddle as it makes for sidings at the foot of the Londonderry incline. Dorman Long relinquished this one also in 1963 for less than four years work at Seaham. (June 1965)

11

Down to the Sea in Trucks — Seaham Harbour

A cold grey sea reflects the coal-dusty port of Seaham over which squats the mining town of Seaham Harbour. Some six miles south of Sunderland and the river Wear, in County Durham, the town and harbour are claimed, along with Middlesbrough, as the first places to be created by the coming of the railways. The north-east claims to be the original coal mining area in the country and also the district in which the major development of the infant steam locomotive took place. South of the Tyne, the coal-field stretched some fifty miles; at its widest part it ran thirty miles in from the coast, and what was once pleasantly wooded countryside and a charming coastline of limestone cliffs, soon became punctured with pits and ramified with railways.

Lord Londonderry, an influential landowner in the district, acquired the Newbottle pits in 1819; these were connected by a waggonway to Fatfield staithes on the Wear and the line was extended to Pittington, some four miles north-east of Durham City. Congestion on the riverside was such that Londonderry sought a new outlet for his coal and ultimately made the decision to build a harbour of his own within striking distance of his pits. It was a bold venture, for there was no natural haven on the inhospitable coastline. For this enterprise a site one mile south of the village of Seaham was finally chosen; here, in 1815, Lord Byron had been married. Construction commenced in 1828 and at the same time a cable worked railway, which tunnelled under Stephenson's Hetton Railway at Copt Hill was begun, in order to connect the Rainton pits with the new harbour. In July 1831 the first coal was shipped from the small port, while later in the decade another waggonway was opened, which ran from pits at Haswell through South Hetton, then down two inclines to the quay, and in 1845 extensions were put in hand to make a total of two docks and two tidal basins. The earliest recorded figures for shipment out of Seaham show that in 1857 it was over three quarters of a million tons, yet despite this, in August 1854 Lord Londonderry had opened his own railway to South Sunderland for the conveyance of coal and goods traffic, and in the following July passenger train services were instituted. Although the Rainton to Seaham, and the Seaham to Sunderland lines were known collectively as the Londonderry Railway it seems that they were always regarded as two separate sections, and what remained of the former was closed in November 1896, while the Seaham to Sunderland line was purchased by the North Eastern Railway in October 1900. Londonderry found it impractical to have all his interests connected to one company and under a private Act in 1898 the Seaham Harbour Dock Company was incorporated, taking over the harbour which then underwent further extensions. It is still one of the few ports in the country to operate under private enterprise, an achievement of which the management is justifiably proud.

North Dock and the outer harbour remained much as they had always been but the transformation of South Dock and the adjacent tidal harbour, then totalling five acres, was an impressive undertaking. Steam navvies were employed to shift the magnesium limestone rock, reduced to manageable size by blasting, thereafter concrete walls thirty feet high were built to enclose the ten acre dock. Access to the dock was afforded by two pairs of hydraulically operated karri-wood lock gates spanning the sixty five feet wide entrance, the outer pairs acting as storm gates. To give the necessary protection from the hazardous seas in rough weather, the Outer Harbour was enclosed by two pre-cast concrete block built breakwaters. Built on indigenous rock, and faced with masonry, these were known as the North Pier (1400 feet, crowned with a lighthouse) and the South Pier (920 feet) respectively. Traditional staithes, dating from past centuries, grew like forests of well cultivated timber sixty feet above the quay, both to the north and to the south on the landward side of the dock. A ravelment of railways, high level, low level, and interconnecting, superimposed themselves overall. Full waggons ran down by gravity on to the staithes, dropping their coal through bottom doors down the spouts into the holds of the colliers, then returning, downwards, to low level sidings. The new South Dock, which had been built by Pearsons of Westminster, was officially opened by the then Prime Minister in November 1905.

The town of Seaham grew in consequence of the new prosperity engendered by the expansion of trade – ten thousand souls in 1900 compared with two thousand sixty years previously – the first 'million tons' landmark was achieved in 1906. Despite a decline during the years of World War I, and immediately after, Seaham Harbour was back to the one and a half million ton mark by 1922 and topped the two million figure five years later. To cope with such a bonanza a further development, the Castlereagh Extension of the South Dock, was commenced in 1923, adding $3\frac{1}{4}$ acres to the surface area. Staithes were again a feature, but this time were constructed of concrete, at first on the western side and finally, in 1939, on the eastern side of the berth. A fairground Big Dipper is as nought when compared with the resulting track layout.

The record year had now been passed, for it was in 1930 that 2,314,530 tons had been handled by this port of modest dimensions. Throughout the whole of World War II it is remarkable that the shipping figures dropped below the million tons in one year only. For twenty years after the cessation of hostilities the average yearly lading was one and a half million tons, but increasing use of oil fuel, North Sea gas and the decline of the steam locomotive has been reflected in the reduction of Seaham's main commodity, and with it the number of ships using the harbour. The enterprising management has sought to regain the former status of the port by introducing loading and unloading facilities for cargoes other than coal and to this end the wooden staithes were demolished in 1972 – though coal still goes coastwise to power stations at Ipswich, the Thames Estuary and Shoreham-by-Sea. Ships loading 3000 tons are regularly handled. Variety is now the essence of livelihood with limestone, coke breeze, sand, scrap steel, timber, logs and steel passing through, albeit in many instances by road transport, though the railway system still has a useful role to play. Waste stone from the local collieries amounts to a million and a half tons each year and is transported in trains and dumped from the cliffs to the south of the town. Much of this stone comes down the self-acting inclines from South Hetton and Eppleton mines. When we had coal fires in our homes this stuff, we thought, was what the coal merchant delivered! The locals still go beachcombing for small pieces of coal, brought up with the stone, as did the Northumbrians, eight hundred years ago, where the coal seams were exposed on the coast.

If the brain has become befuddled by the bandying about of figures in billions, then let us relax and return to the steamy world of the locomotives, for which Seaham Harbour became a byword. Not only was it a mecca for the railway enthusiast, but any man with a good head of steam on his shoulders could find ample pleasure here. The paddle-steamer tug epoch passed into limbo at Seaham. Since 1818 these graceful vessels had towed out and nosed in the colliers at the north-east coal ports, with the last two (operative until 1969) eking out their twilight in these waters. *Eppleton Hall* (built in 1914) came to Seaham from Sunderland in 1964 to join *Reliant* (built 1907), which had taken up similar duties in 1956 when purchased from Newcastle. *Reliant* was the last steam paddle tug to work in Britain, doing so until the end of April 1969 when she made her last tow. Fortunately both have been preserved, *Eppleton Hall* in San Francisco, and *Reliant* at the National Maritime Museum, Greenwich.

Ah! yes, the locomotives: three had come from the Londonderry Railway and were the most famous of them all. Head Wrightson of Thornaby had built No. 16, in 1870, and No. 17, in 1873, looking for all the world like potato roasters with naked vertical boilers perched on a four wheel undercarriage. Notwithstanding their archaic appearance they continued to work on the lighter jobs, such as the harbour repair trains or on the 'gleaning' waggons below the staithes, until 1959 and 1962 respectively, when both retired to their place of birth for preservation. Number 18 was the last of the trio and was the great attraction to steamologists making their pilgrimages to Seaham in the 'sixties. Probably one of the most photographed of all industrial locomotives in the country, its real age, true to feminine form, remains shrouded in mystery. However, recent evidence shows that it probably dates from 1870 rather than the hitherto accepted 1863. Whatever the facts, it outran every last one of the steam stock, even continuing to work after the diesel invasion in 1967. Built in Poole by S. Lewin as a well tank, it was at some stage converted to a saddle tank, and the cab was added: a vital necessity one would have thought when working on the North Pier in a Nor' Easter. The engine crews working on the Head Wrightsons would have needed to be dressed in lifeboatmen's oilskins at such times. It is said that the cab and chimney were transferred from No. 19, a Black Hawthorn 0-4-0ST, also ex-Londonderry Railway. Now languishing in solitary confinement, it awaits the day when it will be restored to public display.

New locomotives were something of a rarity on the harbour system. *Seaton*, designed as an 0-4-4T for the Londonderry Railway, was built at Seaham Works in 1902 as an 0-6-0 tank, and two six-coupled saddle tanks were purchased from Peckett in 1905 and 1906 respectively. On completion of the dock extension in 1905, Pearson sold two four-wheelers, a Manning Wardle and a Hunslet, to be joined by four ancient North Eastern Railway cast-offs, two 0-6-0 tender, and two 0-6-0 saddle tank engines between 1907 and 1911. Before reverting once more to second-hand stock, Hawthorn Leslie supplied two 0-6-0 saddle tanks, *Juno* and *Neptune* in the years 1922 and 1936, and finally in 1956 came two vertical boilered Sentinels. One of these latter was converted five years later to diesel hydraulic propulsion. From then on no less than seventeen hand-me-downs arrived, though two were merely to provide spare parts. The NCB supplied two – a second Number 18 (Black Hawthorn of 1867!) and a Manning Wardle – while five Hawthorn Leslie design 0-4-0 saddle tanks came from Consett Iron Co. Ltd in 1960. The year 1961 saw the arrival of two similar locomotives, for spares, from South Durham Steel & Iron Co. Ltd, with the final eight steamers, all ex Dorman Long & Co. Ltd, two years later. There never was a renumbering scheme and all second-hand purchases retained their original numbers or names, and in some cases livery, though dark green was officially the standard Seaham colour. There was no engine shed, merely a lean-to repair bay, so that locomotives when not in use were scattered about near the dock entrance to the delight of photographers.

In their heyday, Seaham Harbour locomotives would handle trains from the many local collieries. New Seaham Colliery, situated some 200 feet above sea level, was opened about 1859 and later merged with the nearby Seaton Colliery, on the original cable incline from Rainton, with an inclined plane down to the harbour. NCB and dock locomotives formerly worked on the incline by adhesion, while loads of stone came down by cable until 1968 when the line was singled and locomotive working instituted throughout. One mile to the south is Dawdon Colliery, opened in 1907, with direct rail link operated by S.H.D. Company locomotives. Further south are Easington, Horden and Blackhall, all connected by BR as is Vane Tempest, the youngest, which was opened half a mile to the north in 1929. Seams from all these pits are worked under the sea up to six miles out. Small amounts of coal still come 'down the rope' from South Hetton and Eppleton, but thanks to the traffic in colliery waste these are the busiest remaining inclines in the county.

Though coal shipments have decreased, there is still plenty of activity for the Vanguard Sentinel conversion and the five new English Electric Vulcan 0-6-0 diesel-hydraulics built in 1967. Modernization struck Seaham with a jolt, for less than ten years ago the scene could still epitomize the mid-Victorian – the long legged staithes gloomed over the paddlers and over the Lewin with its chaldron waggons, all the last of their breeds. The waggons were no less steeped in history, being 'modern' (*c.*1870) versions of those on eighteenth century Tyneside. Again these had been handed down from the Londonderry Railway and indeed some retained their original owner's numbering until the end. Posterity will be indebted to Seaham for more than *Reliant* and the Lewin, for some of the chaldron waggons and a coal drop are to be displayed at the N.E. Regional Open Air Museum at Beamish.

Industry cannot thrive on sentiment, however, and for those who bemoan the evaporation of Seaham's steam, there is the salutory thought that much of the coal dug and despatched will raise the steam which turbine-generates our electricity.

12 The veteran Lewin number 18 has made two reversals on its way from North Pier to the short tunnel by the North Dock and faces a longer tunnel before gaining the main docks area.

13 The lighthouse holds up an admonishing finger lest No. 18 should stray too far out to sea while a steam crane salutes the old timer at the end of another day's work aiding the vital sea defences to be kept up to scratch. Dump trucks have taken over this job.

14 Piquantly contrasting styles of rolling stock follow the Lewin along the Castlereagh Extension. Note how the outlines of the all steel waggon of almost 10-tons tare follow closely the pattern of the ancient $2\frac{1}{2}$-ton 'black waggon' but with the additional luxury of springs and four-wheel brakes!

15 No. 18 would seem to have a tight squeeze between the staithes' stalks to retrieve the chaldron waggon, there to pick up the coal crumbs which fall from the masters table above. But owing to the tight curves, locomotives were not allowed under the staithes. More powerful locomotives lifted the spillage waggons up to the high level sidings as shown on page 16. (June 1965)

16 Serving Cornwall's 200-year-old China clay industry the port of Par in St Austell Bay was opened c.1840 for the export of tin and copper. Taken over by the English China Clay Company in 1946 it had five miles of sidings with two connections to the London–Penzance main line. *Alfred,* a chubby cheeked Bagnall (3058 of 1953), was built for a loading gauge clearance of 7 ft 6 in. Livery is light green.   (October 1973)

17 Still in Cornwall, though in an even stronger maritime environment, Falmouth Docks and Engineering Co. No. 5 (Hudswell Clarke 1632 of 1929) is sometimes called upon to tow vessels into dock. Oil tank traffic is its usual métier, for Falmouth is a tanker port specializing in repairs to these vessels. Until 1961 this 14 in. × 22 in. cyl. Hudswell Clarke was owned by the Manchester CWS at Irlam.   (October 1973)

18 Chatham dockyard, founded in the reign of Elizabeth I, is remembered as the launching place of Nelson's *Victory,* completed in 1765. The railway came to the dockyard in 1864 and among the last of a long line of land steamers was green liveried *Veday* a typical Andrew Barclay pug (2198 of 1945). Two of Chatham's locomotives have been preserved: *Invicta* at Bridgnorth and *Singapore* at Ashford.   (July 1961)

19 Although No. 4 *Marlborough* was built for the Royal Ordnance Factory at Chorley in Lancs., and in 1958 worked for T. W. Ward in Preston, the final move was to its native land. Supplied by Andrew Barclay in 1940 (Works number 2081) its days ended at Wards shipbreaking yard in Inverkeithing. 64620 an ex. North British Railway 0-6-0, BR class J37, takes on a trainload of scrap metal – a portent of things to come, in 1969, for No. 4.   (September 1966)

18

19

20 Against a backcloth of carefully woven shipyard gantries *Roker* makes for the prefabrication shops of the Doxford & Sunderland Shipbuilding and Engineering Company. *Roker*, with 12 in. × 15 in. cylinders, was built by R. Stephenson & Hawthorn in 1940 (works number 7006) to a 1902 design and was withdrawn in 1971 when the 13-mile rail system closed. *Roker* and *Hendon* were built from parts made for an unfulfilled order in 1918!

21 Unconcerned by the cutter's torch *Millfield* (R. Stephenson & Hawthorn 7070 of 1942) tiptoes into the prefabrication shop. The yard at Pallion was opened in 1840 and to Sunderland goes the credit of being the single British town with the highest output of new ships. Formerly known as Wearmouth, shipbuilding there commenced commercially in 1346.

22 Under the shadow of the Queen Alexandra bridge, over the Wear, nestles the five-road shed which housed five locos! From left to right are saddle tank *General* (Peckett 2049 of 1944 and ex. Morris Motors, Cowley) and crane tanks *Pallion* (Hawthorn Leslie 2517 of 1902); *Millfield*, *Roker* and *Southwick* (R. Stephenson & Hawthorn 7069 of 1942). Not only did they possess steam operated jibs with three fixed hook positions but also a modified version of Joy's valve gear. Note their enormous dumb buffers and unusual position of the lamp bracket. Standard livery was green. Between the years 1902 and 1971 eleven crane engines worked here, five have been preserved.

(September 1969)

21
22

From Ironstone to Steel — Corby

Northamptonshire, a delightful agricultural county in the heart of England, is also bang in the middle of a crescent-shaped area of stratified iron ore fields which stretch from Lincolnshire through Oxfordshire. Although iron is known to have been used in some parts of the world over 3000 years ago, evidence suggests that it was produced in this country from outcropping ore, around 200 BC. The principle centres of smelting by charcoal were Lincolnshire, Rutland, Northamptonshire, Sussex and Kent, but owing to the excessive denuding of forests the art of the smelters eventually died out. Seventeenth century experiments with alternative fuels for the production of iron culminated in success for Abraham Darby, a former Bristol ironmaster, who moved to Coalbrookdale where, in 1709, he made good quality pig-iron by using coke.

Although Northamptonshire had been considered mainly ore-less it was rediscovered during the early part of the nineteenth century and in sufficient quantity for ironworks to be set up at Wellingborough in 1852. Soon this sphere of activity became the second largest ore-mining area in the country – Yorkshire claiming first place – but despite the hope of some industrialists that it might become a second 'Black Country' extensive trial borings through the limestone showed that no coal existed. It was in 1879, when the Midland Railway was building its route from Kettering to Nottingham via Manton that deep deposits of ironstone were exposed in the cutting leading to Corby tunnel. Quarrying began on a large scale in 1882 by the Cardigan Iron Ore Company, in lands owned by Lord Cardigan to the south of Corby village, then numbering some 800 inhabitants. A typical sleepy English hamlet, consisting of a few cottages clustered around the church, together with a few farmsteads, was a century later destined to become a thriving industrial town whose population had increased over sixty-fold. A standard gauge tramway was laid down, with connection to the MR, and worked by a Hunslet Engine Company 0-4-0 saddle tank, built in 1883 and named *Vigilant*. This remarkable little engine has survived through many ownerships up to the present day and is now preserved at Quainton Road, Buckinghamshire. Lloyds Ironstone Company took over the workings in 1885, opening up new quarries in the area, with a second locomotive, again from Hunslet, appropriately named *Ironstone*. The first steam driven mechanical digger to work in the ironstone fields was introduced in 1895 for loading iron-ore on to railway waggons. Hard upon this came the long jib shovels, the 'American Devils' which scooped up the overburden, together with the top soil, and deposited the loads in worked out parts of the quarry. Thus the land could not be reclaimed afterwards, to the detriment of much good agricultural land, yet for fifty years this decimation was allowed to continue until, by Act of Parliament, restoration became compulsory wherever practicable. To this end the coming of the dragline excavators was a boon, for they could skim off

24

23 Sandwiched between the North Exchange sidings and the blast furnaces are two locos. on the slag ladles job. No. 29 (right), a 14 in. outside cylinder Andrew Barclay (1457 of 1915), in black livery eyes with suspicion an interloper from the Minerals Division. On loan to the steelworks from Gretton Brook Depot is No. 54 (R. Stephenson & Hawthorn 7031 of 1941) with its soiled green livery now 'works grey'. No. 29 ceased work for ever in 1967 while 54 later went to the Stour Valley Railway. A lucky shot this. (March 1965)

24 The pulling potential and the strapping lines of No. 56 (R. Stephenson & Hawthorn 7667 of 1950) are well evident here as it drifts down the Harringworth road with plenty of steam (and coal) going to waste. Now with the Kent & East Sussex Railway it should prove a useful acquisition. (November 1965)

the top soil and set it aside for later rehabilitation.

Until 1910, quarrying the ore, for use at Wellingborough Ironworks, among others, was the sole activity of the Company at Corby, and it was then that two blast furnaces were erected near the site of the original workings. During World War I extensions of the railway system to new quarries in the east, north and north-west of the area took place. Meanwhile the first of a long line of six-coupled locomotives had been put into traffic. Stewarts & Lloyds Ltd, a tube making concern formed by the amalgamation, in 1903, of Lloyds & Lloyds of Birmingham and Stewarts & Menzies of Glasgow, twenty years later acquired a controlling interest in Lloyds Ironstone Co. Ltd, whereupon large scale development was planned, not only through the take-over of other quarries in the county but for the construction of a new iron, steel and tube manufacturing Works. Scenes reminiscent of the pioneering railway days when the main lines were being built and shanty towns overflowing with Scots and Irish navvies spread across the landscape, now transformed the environs of a once peaceful village into phantasmagoria. Along with the Works construction went the building of two thousand houses, but before the new heavy industry complex opened in 1934 steelworkers from north of the border were streaming to Corby for jobs. The great steel rush was on. The village church was now dwarfed by a surrealist skyline of furnaces, chimneys, gasholders and pylons, while on the ground the twin-steel tracks of the permanent way twisted their path among acres of long dark sheds and miles of sidings. From a new loco shed within the Works, steam locomotives trailed their white woolly exhausts to all points of the compass under a tangled knitwear of pipes and gantries, or out into the verdant, wooded countryside. Black, brown and yellow smoke, mingling with the stark steam stippling, etched kaleidoscopic clouds across the sky. The name of Corby became indelibly inscribed upon the map.

With the erection of the original blast furnaces, locomotives specifically for ironworks duties began to arrive, the first from Andrew Barclay of Kilmarnock, while many later ones were second-hand, so that by the time the new development was under construction two fleets, embracing the products of Peckett, Hudswell Clarke, Hunslet, Hawthorn Leslie, Manning Wardle and Yorkshire Engine Company, were in co-existence. A *status quo* prevailed after the new shed was built, but at the same time six large 0-6-0 saddle tanks with 16 in. × 24 in. outside cylinders were purchased from Hawthorn Leslie of Newcastle for employment around the Works. This was a standard design of the builders, more familiar perhaps in the collieries of north-east England, and its choice may have been attributed to the experience gained with a similar machine which had come to Corby from the North Lincolnshire Iron Co. Ltd in 1931. From then on, these fine locomotives became entrenched and until the day that steam was ruled out of court every new (discounting second-hand) addition, with one last exception, was of this type. Four more arrived in 1936, another one in 1938, followed by one in each of the years 1940 and 1941, these two latter from Robert Stephenson & Hawthorn Ltd (successors to Hawthorn Leslie). Hunslet had supplied the first locomotive to Corby in 1883 and it was fitting that the last new steam locomotive to be purchased by the steelworks was from that same Company, although in rather curious circumstances. After the outbreak of World War II Stewarts & Lloyds considered making a rail connection between Corby Works and their ironworks at Islip, near Thrapston. Eight large six-coupled saddle tanks with 18 in. × 26 in. inside cylinders were designed and built to Stewarts & Lloyds specification, by the Hunslet Engine Co. Ltd but the Islip project fell by the wayside. In the event only the first of the class, known as the '50550', went to Corby.

Whereas the steel division favoured the Hawthorn Leslie design, the minerals side had opted for Manning Wardles with 16 in. × 22 in. inside cylinders, though there were one or two exceptions. This design was perpetuated by Kitson & Co. and by Robert Stephenson & Hawthorn after the demise of Manning Wardle in 1927. A total of fifteen such locomotives was built for Stewarts & Lloyds between 1910 and 1941, though they took part in some interchange between Corby and other quarries in the group. Post-war, came the only ex-main-line engine to ply about the Works. No. 27, a 'puggie', had been built by the Caledonian Railway in 1902 at Glasgow, serving the LMS and then a colliery in Lanarkshire before coming south. It would be remarkable, nay ironic, if it had not been driven by a Scot at Corby!

The year 1949 saw the commencement of further expansion and improvements to the industrial complex and at the same time Corby, which had become an Urban District in 1939, was designated a 'New Town' with its own Development Corporation. From a population of 1600 in 1932, it had expanded to the tune of 13,000, which doubled during the next ten years and by the early 'seventies was 50,000. The new town to the west of the 'village' was laid out in no Victorian manner of chess board streets cramped by closely packed terraces, nor was it allowed to get submerged under a vast uniform housing estate. Natural features, such as wooded areas were retained, with the neat dwellings built around them on wide roads with spacious tree lined green verges. Pleasing red brick shopping centres and civic buildings steered away from egg-box construction common to so many redevelopment schemes of recent years. Though the heat and smoke of the working day are an unpleasant and unavoidable part of the environment, a chance to get away from it all is afforded the artisans during their well earned leisure. Despite the continued growth in other directions, one civilized amenity is now missing – the main line railway station!

A locomotive renumbering scheme had taken place in 1936 whereby 1 to 30 became the steelworks fleet, and 31 upwards the quarry locomotives. Although Stewarts & Lloyds Minerals Ltd was formed as a separate entity in 1950, the locomotives still shared the same shed at the Works. Almost immediately, the new Company took delivery of some powerful tailor made 18 in. × 26 in. inside cylinder 0-6-0 saddle tanks from Stephenson & Hawthorns. When the first of these arrived it was in a new light green livery with red side rods, soon to be applied to all the Mineral's locomotives, which had hitherto been black, as were the steelworks engines. Concurrently, a decision was taken to adopt a yellow warning livery for the Works fleet, which considering their stygian surroundings was not likely to remain pristine for long but if, and when, clean they were more readily visible to men working in close proximity to the track. As it turned out not all of the stock was so treated.

Harringworth pits, formerly isolated (using narrow gauge tramways) being some five miles north of Corby, were connected to the main system in 1952 and twelve years later were extended another couple of miles to Wakerley Dock. Here the ore is brought by road dumpers for transfer to 30-ton hopper waggons. Double track has been installed with colour light signals at junctions where the lines diverge to other quarries *en route*. Totalling forty route miles, this was the largest ironstone system in the country. Meanwhile a large brick built locomotive shed, with roller shutter doors, having eight tracks capable of housing forty locomotives was opened at Gretton Brook, about one mile north of the Works, in 1954, and sometimes erroneously known as Pen Green depot. To this sumptuous edifice came the rolling stock of S & L Minerals, and as the average allocation was twenty five they would hibernate at weekends spaced widely apart, chimneys to the east. Two were left behind and joined the steelworks stud. Midway betwixt shed and Works lie the North Bank reception sidings where Minerals engines deposit loaded trains and return with empties to the quarries. Steelworks locomotives were rarely allowed to venture north of this point. A colour bar had set in. Not entirely, for there were periods when the Minerals

25 Odd man out at Gretton Brook was No. 39 *Rhos* the sole Hudswell Clarke (1308 of 1915) frequently employed on the permanent way train, seen here skirting the Tarmac Plant, on the approach to Weldon Road bridge. This 15 in. × 22 in. outside cylinder locomotive is now in private hands. (November 1964)

26 Weak winter sun highlights the exhaust from No. 44 *Conway* (Kitson 5469 of 1933) courageously thumping upgrade from Earlstrees quarry. *Conway* was one of six Manning Wardle design 16 in. × 22 in. inside cylinder locomotives built by Kitsons at Leeds for Stewarts & Lloyds and since the demise of steam at Gretton Brook has become a museum piece. (December 1964)

27

28

locos were loaned to the steelworks, or when the platelayer's train was required occasionally to help out on the Works system; and once, a yellow Hawthorn newly converted to burn oil was tested over the quarry lines. Seven of the fourteen Hawthorns, plus the big Hunslet were fitted for oil firing during 1960 to 1962.

New pits to the south-east and south-west of the Works were opened up in the late 'fifties employing 'walking draglines' 1650 tons with 27-ton capacity buckets. The 30-ton capacity bucket draglines have since been introduced, with 300 foot jibs. To gain North Bank reception, trains from these quarries run over part of the line connecting the Works with the main line interchange sidings south of Corby, then swing round to the east, circumnavigating the edge of the Works area, and finally approaching North Bank sidings from the opposite point of the compass! Working up gradients as high as 1 in 70 from the quarry floor meant that trains would need a locomotive both fore and aft. Often these would be two of the '56' class, as the Stephenson & Hawthorn engines became known. Ten locomotives formed this class, seven built in 1950, one in 1954 and two in 1958, the last of which was delivered to Harlaxton quarries, Lincolnshire. Headlights, operated by Stone's steam generators, were fitted at the base of the chimneys and at the rear of the cabs, for working early on winter mornings when most of us were still abed.

On a cold foggy day in January 1969, the fires were dropped for the last time at Gretton Brook, when No. 44 *Conway* and No. 56 completed a round trip from Wakerley Dock with an Industrial Railway Society special train, less than eight years after the first diesel had run on the Minerals' system. Likewise the last steamer at the steelworks, No. 21, made its final bow on an IRS tour over the same tracks in June 1973. It had taken twenty-eight years for diesels to oust the steam locomotives from the Works! Nowadays there are some thirty-three diesels allocated to the Steel Division and twenty-seven at the Minerals depot still wearing the traditional yellow and green liveries respectively.

There was a time when one could sit by the Harringworth 'road' amid butterflies and buttercups, out of sight and sound of the sulphurated hubbub of the Corby inferno, idling the time away in patience for the vociferous bark of a '56' blasting upwards. Now the twilight has gone; only the reverberations of a Rolls Royce Sentinel drown the song of the blackbird.

27 Another Stephenson & Hawthorn 18 in. locomotive, adding a contribution to an already overburdened sky, shunts North Bank Ore Reception sidings. No. 57 (R.S.&H. 7668 of 1950) is one of three similar machines now employed on the Keighley & Worth Valley Railway where they operate passenger trains with ease on the 1 in 60 grades. (November 1965)

28 At the Tarmac Plant No. 6, formerly *Ironworks No. 2*, (Andrew Barclay 1242 of 1911) indulges in a spot of shunting while in the distance No. 24 (Hunslet 2411 of 1941) the fugitive from the ill-fated Islip scheme, with a string of 'Long Tube' empties from the South Exchange sidings, takes on water. (March 1965)

29 No. 38 *Dolobran*, the pioneer Manning Wardle of the Minerals Division (1762 of 1912), marches away from Cowthick Quarry south-west of Corby *en route* to North Bank. The setting belies its proximity to the giant industrial complex. No. 38 is also preserved on the Kent & East Sussex Railway while another five of the class, including both Kitson and R.S.&H. examples, are well cared for in various locations. (March 1965)

30 One of the seven oil burning Hawthorn Leslie design saddle tanks drawing a train of empty slag ladles for the blast furnaces, with the coke ovens in the far background. This shows clearly the altered bunker for liquid fuel. 14 (Hawthorn Leslie 3827 of 1934) with its 'buttercup and wasp' livery as yet untarnished by oil and grime now resides in the childrens playground at West Glebe Park, wearing a livery of dark green embellished with aerosol graffiti. (May 1966)

31 Stewarts & Lloyds also have a Tube Works at Newport (Mon.), now part of the British Steel Corporation empire, where four-wheeled Andrew Barclays once ruled the roost. *Drake*, No. 2086, an oil burner, was built in 1940 for the Royal Ordnance Factory, Glascoed. The 1906 transporter bridge across the Usk river straddles the background. *Drake* has since gone to Ashchurch for preservation. (November 1969)

32 Iron ore was 'rediscovered' at Scunthorpe in 1859 Frodingham ironworks came into blast in 1865. Since then three steelworks (Appleby Frodingham; John Lysaght; and Guest Keen & Baldwins) became established. Here at the Redbourn works of G.K.B. a Hunslet (3813 of 1953) 18 in. inside cylinder saddle tank of class '48150' appears to be lost on a space-rocket launching pad. No. 18, formerly *Redbourn 30*, was cut up in 1970. (October 1965)

33 Workington's first recorded ironworks was opened in 1858 though coking coal was imported from County Durham, the local coal being unsuitable. The present scale of operations grew from the amalgamation of four companies in 1909 to become the Workington Iron & Steel Co. No. 73 (R. Stephenson & Hawthorn 7048 of 1942) performs at Moss Bay Works prior to transfer to the NCB in 1967 and the cutter's torch the following year.

34 On the slag ladles run a pugnacious 18 in. six-wheeler climbs above the long buried eighteenth century Lady Pit, Chapel Bank Pit and the waggonway. Two four-wheeled bogies carry the ladles which were operated by a steam pipe from the buffer beam of the locomotive. Built to a 1934 Robert Stephenson & Co. Ltd design No. 78 (R. Stephenson & Hawthorn 7946 of 1959) was withdrawn in 1967, when steam ceased at the steelworks, and scrapped in 1970. (August 1965)

35 A familiar figure for some years was the gateman at Riddings Foundry closing the A613 Alfreton road for *Stanton No. 36* to pass into the Works yard. Edward Oakes established his ironworks here in 1792. It was taken over by the Stanton Ironworks Co. in 1921 and closed seven years later. The foundry remained open until 1969. The locomotive was built by Andrew Barclay in 1937 (Works number 2042) and scrapped in 1970.

36 *Stanton No. 36* bundles a train into the exchange sidings at Riddings. Stanton slipped up in 'naming' two locomotives *Stanton No. 36*. Both were Barclays, though the one at Stanton Works was a bigger six-coupled machine. (September 1967)

37 North of Chesterfield at Staveley village a forge was in existence in 1608, and the first coke furnace was set up in 1786. 1863 saw the formation of the Staveley Coal & Iron Co. and the subsequent building of the Devonshire Ironworks. Under a hundred year agreement with the Midland Railway, in 1866, that company's locomotives shunted about the ironworks. In the year before the agreement ceased No. 41835, built in 1892 for the MR by Vulcan Foundry (works number 1365), was captured with a rake of 'internal use only' waggons.

38 Twin souls at Staveley contemplate the next move. No. 41804 (built at Derby in 1890) spent forty five years on this duty while 41835 distinguished itself by acquiring a Belpaire boiler as late as 1961. Five of a former total of 280 locomotives, designed by S. W. Johnson in 1874, remained until 1965 when the agreement expired. Only 41708 has been preserved. (April 1964)

37
38

35

39 Pecketts had a grace all their own but, like children, the bigger they grew the less enchanting they became. *B.A.Co.*2 coyly hides its charms at the Burntisland (Fifeshire) Works of British Aluminium, opened in 1915. Main line locomotives bring in train loads of African bauxite from the docks and carry away the oxide to aluminium refineries in the West Highlands. Peckett 1579 of 1921 is a 10 in. × 15 in. cylindered M5 class in green livery becoming preserved in 1972 at Hereford and named *Pectin*. (June 1965)

40 Another M5 Peckett (1903 of 1936) shows off its graceful feminine lines, somewhat marred by a spark arrester, ambling along by the mouth of the River Ely while the capital of the Principality sprawls ungainly across the background. Penarth Docks were opened by the Taff Vale Railway in 1865 as a coal exporting port. South Wales Warehouses Ltd declared the Peckett redundant in 1968, later being purchased for private preservation. (October 1968)

41 Difficult to believe that this diminutive, long necked, Hudswell Clarke (works number 1882) was built, at Leeds, in 1955. Named *Mirvale* it had a relatively short working life at the Mirfield (Yorks) plant of the Mirvale Chemical Co. for in 1969 it found a new home with the North Yorkshire Moors Railway at Grosmont. (May 1967)

40

41

42 The grandiose title of Bradford Corporation Water Pollution Control Department sounds much sweeter than Esholt Sewage Works which at one time had a maximum of twenty track miles with ten locomotives to work in surroundings much more pleasant than the name suggests. Sections of the system could be seen from the carriage window near Apperley viaduct when travelling between Leeds and Bradford on the old Midland line, or from the Leeds and Liverpool Canal. The locomotive is *Elizabeth* another late Hudswell Clarke product (1888 of 1958). (September 1969)

43 *Elizabeth* and *Nellie* showing the art of gentle persuasion to a load of sludge waggons. *Nellie* was also a local lass from Hudswell Clarke (Works No. 1435) being born in 1922. She is now in a nearby museum. When the diesels arrived *Elizabeth* was relegated to the role of stand-by engine.

44 *Nellie* is left to fend for itself among some less-than-salubrious surroundings at Esholt. Both locomotives were once equipped to burn wool grease recovered from sewage fed by Holden liquid fuel burning apparatus. In about 1967 they were converted to normal oil firing. *Nellie* is a 14 in. × 20 in. cylinder locomotive; *Elizabeth* 14 in. × 22 in.   (March 1969)

Steam Under the City

Where does one draw the line between Industrial and Main Line locomotives? The answer can be ambiguously woolly, for the line is by no means straight and has been crossed with impunity from both sides. All main line companies possessed four- or six-wheel tank locomotives for Works, or for dockyard duties, some of which were built to the standard designs of the private locomotive building firms who supplied similar engines to industry. On the other hand there were many types of both tender and tank engines, specifically designed for main line work, which when they had run their allotted span were purchased by industry for a further lease of useful life. One need only cite the LBSCR *Terriers* as an obvious example, for they were built as suburban passenger locomotives and, in several cases, ended up in dockyards, colliery and ironstone workings. A similar, but lesser known parallel, was the sale of some Metropolitan Railway 4-4-0 tank engines which had spent the first thirty years, or more, of their lives ferreting around under the streets of London.

The Metropolitan, brainchild of one Charles Pearson, M.P. had been built after thirty years of opposition, apathy and legal wrangling to bring railways into the heart of the City. Initially a line of $3\frac{3}{4}$ miles from Paddington to Farringdon Street was constructed and brought into use in the remarkably short time of three years. John Fowler, the Company's engineer, had the unenviable task of excavating the clay, sand and gravel, while diverting underground rivers and sewers from the path. It was all 'cut' but not all 'cover', for part of the line was in a deep cutting open to the sky, thereby affording much needed ventilation for the steam locomotives, their drivers and passengers alike. Pearson had envisaged the interconnection of the existing main line railways via one vast exchange station in the centre of the Metropolis, but opposition was so intense that nothing came of these far sighted proposals. However, some railway companies were so aware of the advantages to themselves inherent in the finally accepted scheme that the Great Western became a substantial shareholder and agreed to operate the line. The Great Northern, though interested, would not part with cash but merely sat back and waited. Despite this, a standard gauge connection was built to the GNR from the dual gauge Metropolitan at Kings Cross. The GWR, of course, was then 7 ft $0\frac{1}{4}$ in. gauge.

During the years of construction, commencing in 1860, the true industrial locomotive of the contractors worked on the line while Fowler set about designing a 'smokeless engine' which resulted in a 2-4-0 outside cylinder tender locomotive built by Robert Stephenson & Co. Ltd. Although this produced little smoke, it also produced little steam, so that public services opened in January 1863 were worked by GWR Gooch outside cylinder 2-4-0 condensing well tanks. This was short lived. Disputes soon arose between the Metropolitan and the Great Western who withdrew its trains in the following August. It was now the turn of the overjoyed Great Northern who took over the traffic with tender engines hastily fitted with condensers. Six years later the broad gauge disappeared from the 'Met'.

Meanwhile, Beyer Peacock of Manchester had in 1864 supplied to the Metropolitan the first batch of what was to become the standard 'underground' locomotive, the condensing 4-4-0T of class A, which with the similar class B, eventually grew to 66 examples by 1885. The precursor of the class was the first to be withdrawn in 1897 for scrapping but later, five of them went back to grass roots, working in coalfields. South Hetton Colliery Co. rebuilt one as a 0-6-0T which lasted until 1948 (as did two at Pelaw Main) the year after the coal industry was nationalized. London Transport withdrew the sole survivor on home territory in the same year. In this case the locomotive was preserved and is now on display in the London Transport Museum at Brentford. Built in 1866, it had served on passenger trains until 1935, latterly on the rural Brill branch in Buckinghamshire, ending its days on Works trains around Neasden.

No sooner had the world's first underground passenger railway become established than a second was projected. The Metropolitan District, or District for short, was of two miles length, from Kensington to Westminster. It was opened in 1868, and connected with the Metropolitan at the jointly owned station of South Kensington. Train services were worked by the Metropolitan until 1871 by which time the District had been extended to Blackfriars. In that year the District introduced its own locomotives, the Beyer Peacock 4-4-0T design and eventually, by 1886, fifty-four were in service, all of which survived until the days of electrification. Both railways were intent on expanding as far and as rapidly as possible and although the majority of shareholders felt that they should amalgamate, the rival chairmen, Edward Watkin (Metropolitan) and James Forbes (District) could not agree terms. Such was the antagonism between the two that the final connection which completed the thirteen mile Inner Circle route was delayed until 1884.

Services had commenced over the Widened Lines in the same year that the District was opened; these

45 Railways superseded the canals in the transport business after the 'Railway Mania' of the 1840s but fifty years previously a similar mania had smitten the canal builders. Authorized in 1793 the Grand Junction Canal was cut from Brentford, on the Thames, to Buckby in Northants. where it joined the Leicestershire & Northamptonshire Canal. By an amalgamation of nine canals in 1929 it became known as the Grand Union Canal and as such was Britain's longest. Near Watford, L90 (ex. GWR 7760) built by the North British Loco. Co. Ltd (24048 of 1930) barges along with a spoil train for Croxley tip. (November 1969)

being independent tracks over which Great Northern Railway and Midland Railway trains ran into Moorgate Street station. From Kings Cross (Metropolitan) the line ran eastwards along the north side of the Metropolitan Railway, then burrowed underneath the Ray Street 'Grid Iron' to the south, thence via Farringdon terminating at Moorgate, which had been opened by the Met in 1865. The London Chatham & Dover Railway also ran to Farringdon from 1866 to 1907 (a Moorgate service operated until 1916) and main line steam suburban trains continued working from Moorgate to the former GNR and MR lines until displaced under the BR diesel programme. Pearson's dreams had been to some extent fulfilled, for although his great interchange station never became a reality, through passenger and freight services across London became established. Not only that, but freight depots were now more centrally situated, having access by rail from the outside world. These were the City Goods Depot (GNR), Whitecross Street (MR) and the GWR Smithfield depot, access to which was gained from Paddington along the original Metropolitan line. What Pearson could never have visualized was that the London commuter system would eventually total some 250 route miles and at its furthest point was, at one time, fifty miles north-west from the centre of the Capital.

Electric traction first came to the Underground in 1890 with the opening of the City & South London Railway, which was followed by five more tunnelled railways. Realizing that they would have to electrify the Inner Circle, or lose traffic, the Metropolitan and the District conducted trials between Earls Court and Kensington in 1899. However, old rivalries died hard and they were soon at loggerheads once more in deciding which particular system should be adopted. It was, therefore, September 1905 before the last steam train trailed its smoke out of the Inner Circle.

Steam was still going strong on a number of suburban routes and on the main line, from Harrow to Quainton Road, which was shared with the Great Central. It was not until 1961 that the last steam hauled passenger train service was withdrawn, on the section between Rickmansworth and Aylesbury, and although this had been operated from 1937 with LNER motive power hauling London Transport stock, which had come down from the City with electric locomotives, some of the old Met engines were at times called on to deputize.

Between the abolition of steam from the Underground and its final extinction on passenger work there had been two significant events. The first, in 1933, was the setting up of the London Passenger Transport Board which assumed control of the Underground railways, the trams and buses alike. Less than fifteen years later, in January 1948, the LPTB became nationalized under the London Transport Executive. Steam continued to flourish on the maintenance, stores and spoil trains until 6 June 1971 when the last three locomotives were withdrawn. A special Works train was run from Moorgate to Neasden to mark the occasion, whereupon the stations *en route* were crammed with sightseers in excess of the weekday rush hour crowds; while Neasden depot, open to the public, witnessed scenes reminiscent of Cup Final day at Wembley. London Transport steam evaporated in a cloud of glory to match steam's necrosis on British Railways almost three years previously.

For all its function as an intensive passenger railway there was, from the days of expansion into the suburbs, a substantial goods traffic to be carried, together with the very necessary maintenance trains which were mainly the preserve of steam locomotives. Apart from those Beyer Peacocks which went into industrial service four of the five Metropolitan 2-4-0 tanks, built by Sharp Stewart in 1894, were sold for a similar purpose. London Transport did, however, use some genuine industrial types of its own. Those well remembered, for they were not withdrawn until the early 1960s, were two outside cylinder Hunslet 0-6-0 side tanks, of a class familiar in the Manchester district collieries, (formerly District stock) and two ex-Metropolitan inside cylinder 0-6-0 saddle tanks of Peckett's standard class X. The former were stabled at Lillie Bridge depot, near Earl's Court, and the latter at Neasden. In earlier years Manning Wardle had been represented by three 0-6-0ST class K; with a Hudswell Clarke 0-4-0ST working on the Met; the District was host to a Kerr Stuart 0-4-2ST, while the Central London Railway had two oil-burning Hunslet 0-6-0 tanks.

The largest number and best known locomotives to be used solely on 'industrial' workings were thirteen of the former Great Western Railway's 5700 class 0-6-0 pannier tanks. One of the most numerous to be built in this country, they were introduced in 1929 for shunting and short haul freight trains, though passenger duties were not beneath their dignity! In all, 852 examples were built, the last of which emerged from Swindon in 1950. A further eleven, of like dimensions but fitted with condensing apparatus, were built at Swindon in 1933; they were no strangers on the Underground for they were

46 Three of a kind at Neasden depot. The Metropolitan Railway 'E' class 0-4-4Ts numbered seven in all, three of which were built in the company's Works at Neasden, originally for passenger traffic north of Rickmansworth. L44 formerly Met. No. 1 (Neasden 1896), L46 formerly Met. 77 (Neasden 1896) and L48 formerly Met. 81 (Hawthorn Leslie 2476 of 1901) were $17\frac{1}{2}$ in. × 26 in. cylindered engines and withdrawn in 1964, 1962 and 1963 respectively. L44 is preserved at Quainton Road appropriately enough by the London Railway Preservation Society. (July 1959)

47 In 1901 the Yorkshire Engine Co. Ltd of Sheffield built four 0-6-2T for freight workings on the Metropolitan. On a ballast train is L52, originally Met. 93 (Y.E. works No. 627) at Harrow-on-the-Hill in 'Metroland' formerly Metropolitan/Great Central Railway Joint line. L52 was broken-up at Neasden in 1964. (August 1958)

48 A genuine industrial design was L53, erstwhile Met. 101, from Peckett (664 of 1897) and displaying many of that company's early features, including Salter balance safety valves. The Metropolitan set up its locomotive works at Neasden in 1885 until 1937 when they were rebuilt to make provision for stabling electric stock. It was here that L53 met its ultimate doom in 1960.
(November 1958)

49

intended specifically for the Paddington to Smithfield meat trains. Of the thirteen purchased by London Transport between 1956 and 1963 five had been built by the GWR; five by the North British Loco, Co. Ltd, Glasgow; two at Stoke-on-Trent by Kerr Stuart; and the remaining one by Armstrong Whitworth of Newcastle. When repairs became necessary they were despatched to Swindon Works but later, when Swindon ceased to overhaul steam locomotives, they found their way to Eastleigh Works near Southampton. In the main, they were nocturnal creatures employed during the wee small hours when the underground trains were in bed.

To GWR supporters the red livery of London Transport, which had first appeared on the Met in 1885, must have seemed sacrilegious, but to those of more catholic taste the colour was most acceptable. Five of the number, together with others which saw only GWR service, have been preserved, and in at least one case the London Transport livery has been restored – though this locomotive works in Yorkshire! It seems singularly fitting that the last steam locomotives to work on London's own railway were of Great Western origin for it was with the same Company's locomotives, more than a century before, that the very first service was run.

49 Ray Street Grid Iron in Central London where the widened lines, used by Midland Railway and Great Northern Railway trains, dived under the Metropolitan, making connection between outer suburbia and terminal platforms at Moorgate Street. L95 with a permanent-way train from Neasden (entailing a reversal at Farringdon) loiters around relaying works while a westbound Circle Line train chases the ghost of a Beyer Peacock into the tunnel.
(May 1968)

50 Built by the GWR at Swindon in 1929 as No. 5764, pannier tank L95 trips gaily away from Lillie Bridge depot of the former District Railway in Kensington. A clinically silver snake slithers below oblivious to the steamer making for Northfields. L95, restored in GWR livery, now works along the Severn Valley Railway in Shropshire.
(February 1970)

51 During the invasion of Neasden on D-Day 6th June 1971 (D for demise), L90, like a caged animal, paced up and down with a few waggons for the benefit of those lucky photographers who could get within target range. Fortunately there was no-one south of Chiswick Park station to baulk this shot of a permanent way train returning to Lillie Bridge from Ealing. Even the children on the see-saw did not appreciate what they were missing in the shape of former GWR 7760 which later went to Tyseley to keep L94 company. (April 1968)

52 Greater London steam did not disappear altogether with the withdrawal of the three surviving London Transport pannier tanks. Small pockets of resistance were to be found at a handful of electricity generating stations like Acton Lane, Harlesden, where a characteristically square-shouldered Andrew Barclay *Little Barford* (No. 2069 of 1939) clumps over the Grand Union Canal.   (January 1966)

53 Hudswell Clarke No. 1672 of 1937 with a home-made water carrier settles the summer dust at CEGB Stuart Street Power Station in Manchester. At the time of nationalization almost the entire output of electricity was produced from coal fired stations but by 1971 this had declined to 73 per cent.   (August 1968)

54 Geordies gannin' along the Scotswood Road now only see Stella South Power Station where Blaydon races used to take place. With the bit between its teeth No. 21 (R. Stephenson & Hawthorn 7796 of 1954) canters down the home straight. In the foreground is the BR line (opened in 1835) which four miles farther on passes Wylam where Geo. Stephenson was born, though his birthplace is just across the Tyne in Northumberland. No. 21 is now preserved.   (April 1967)

53

54

King Coal the First

In Northumberland, and along the Firth of Forth, coal was first gathered from seams exposed on the sea shore and its use as an industrial fuel was apparent in the thirteenth century. Newcastle soon became the centre of the trade, shipping coal to London for limeburning, and even cultivated an export business with the continent. During the early years of the next century small scale winning of coal by quarrying spread to other coal-bearing districts in the United Kingdom, while the Northumberland–Durham mining area expanded rapidly. Quarrying gave way to the sinking of pits with the attendant problem of drainage, not successfully overcome until the eighteenth century development of the Newcomen steam pumping engines. By this time coal had at last become acceptable as a domestic fuel and London alone was consuming half a million tons annually. Industries, such as glass-making and smelting, turned from wood burning to the use of coal and began to gravitate to the vicinity of the coalfields, while more docks were required in new, or existing, ports to deal with the export trade.

Not only were the manufacturing industries expanding, but new outlets came into being with the advent of steam locomotives, steam ships and gas production. The year 1812 was one of great import in that Henry Bell's steam tug began operating on the Clyde; Murray's locomotives commenced working the Middleton Colliery railway, and the London & Westminster Chartered Gas Light and Coke Company was founded.

Horse operated railways had begun in the coal industry, and as the latter grew the railways increased in length and number, though not all collieries (true even to this day) had surface railway systems. Underground railways for conveying newly cut coal to the bottom of the pit shaft were introduced in the mid-eighteenth century by the end of which time the underground, narrow gauge, waggons were hoisted on platforms to connect with similar tracks on the surface. With the introduction of steam motive power, greater tonnages could be shifted from the pit heads to the docks, in some cases (especially in Co. Durham) on lengthy and extensive railway systems. Later, when the main line railways network covered the country, colliery locomotives, apart

55 One of the departments of the National Coal Board is that known as National Smokeless Fuels Ltd which, in the main, administers the coking plants.

No one would suspect from this pleasantly pastoral panorama by the banks of the Derwent that within a radius of a mile or so is a coking plant, the industrial centre of Blaydon and the Tyne. Derwenthaugh depot supplies locomotives to work a $2\frac{1}{2}$ mile line to Clockburn Drift Mine to the south and to the coke ovens midway. No. 58 (Vulcan Foundry 5299 of 1945) an Austerity class, modified with a rounded cab for working the tunnel at Lambton Staithes, was ex. WD 75309, later Lambton Hetton & Joicey Collieries and finally NCB owned. It was the last steam locomotive to work at Derwenthaugh, after transfer from Philadelphia in 1969. (September 1969)

56 Norwood coke ovens at Dunston-on-Tyne, formerly the Team By-Products Coke Co. Ltd employs a Stephenson & Hawthorn 16 in. six wheeled saddle tank No. 77 to shunt the yard. (Works number 7412 of 1948). Not surprisingly many of the locomotives used in the local were from this maker, right on the doorstep. (June 1967)

57 An aerial ropeway crosses the former Lancashire & Yorkshire Railway line, from Methley to Pontefract, near Glasshoughton Coking Plant seen from the cab of *Coal Products* No. 3 (Hawthorn Leslie 3575 of 1923).

(October 1974)

from shunting duties, hauled loaded trains to transfer sidings sometimes up to five miles distant, returning to the colliery yards with empty waggons. In the early days of steam the locomotives were built by the coal owners, a practice which survived on a small scale until late in the century. Although scores of suitable main line locomotives came second-hand to the collieries, the mainstay lay in the products of the two hundred-odd British engine-building firms. Quite the commonest types were the 0-4-0 and 0-6-0 tank engines, but the 4-4-0, 0-4-2, 0-4-4, 0-6-2 and 0-8-0 tank types were sometimes employed. Of the few tender engines, the 0-6-0 was favourite, but 0-4-2 and even 2-6-0 were not ignored. Industry employed the first articulated Garratt type locomotive to work in this country, two of which were later built for colliery service.

It is a moot point, which can now never be proved, as to whether it was the coal industry or the building contractors who owned the largest aggregate total of industrial steam locomotives. Whatever the case, they certainly numbered in their thousands.

58 Lambton Staithes as viewed through the ornate 1879 North Eastern Railway bridge. In 1815 a six-mile waggon-way from Newbottle pits ran to staithes on the south bank of the Wear. J. G. Lambton, bought the pits and extended the waggonway in 1822 when contemporaneously Geo. Stephenson's Hetton railway reached the river with staithes upstream of Lambton's. These were linked together by rail in 1911. The staithes, which at one time handled 45,000 tons of coal weekly, were closed in January 1967. (August 1966)

59 Lambton Collieries, with 70 miles of railways, amalgamated with the Hetton Coal Co. in 1911 and again, in 1924, with James Joicey forming the Lambton Hetton & Joicey Collieries Ltd. The hub of the Lambton system is Philadelphia where the main locomotive sheds and Works are situated. Steam working ceased in 1969. Leaving Philadelphia, past the loco sheds on its way to Penshaw marshalling sidings is 42. Built by Robert Stephenson & Co. Ltd in 1920 (Works No. 3801), 42 was scrapped in 1970. (August 1967)

60 Authority was granted in 1864 for the Earl of Durham's locomotives to run over the North Eastern Railway from Penshaw to Sunderland South Dock (opened 1850), and in the following year to Lambton Staithes via Pallion Jnc and the small bore tunnel. It was on account of this that the locomotives had modified cabs. Two and a half miles east of Pallion Junction is Hendon Jnc, hard by the docks, where No. 31, an 0-6-2T with 19 in. × 22 in. cylinders, by Kitson (4533 of 1907) leaves a smudge across a cirrocumulus sky. 31 was broken up in 1968. (August 1966)

61 On the cliffs, two miles north of Blyth, was Cambois Colliery, closed in 1968, where No. 33 (Vulcan Foundry 5303 of 1945) passes a solidly built North Eastern Railway signal box. Austerity class 33 which started life as WD 75313, was sold to the Hartley Main Collieries in 1946. It was renumbered 32 in 1965 and scrapped in 1969.
62 Perched precariously on the skyline is No. 33 at the disposal point near North Blyth where waste stone brought up at Cambois Colliery was dumped on the beach. A loaded train, jogged along by the massive No. 18, (R. Stephenson & Hawthorn 7888 of 1957) an 18 in. × 24 in. outside cylinder saddle tank, passes a North Eastern Railway slotted post signal. No. 18 was broken up when still in knee breeches at the tender age of eleven.
63 Three miles inland and five miles north-east of Newcastle lies Backworth. Just away to the east are Killingworth and West Moors, tangible reminders of the pioneering spirit of George Stephenson. In direct descent is
R. Stephenson & Hawthorn 7166 (built 1944 as WD 71512), fitted with a Hunslet Underfeed Stoker, making the ascent from Whitehill Point Staithes near North Shields on its four mile slog up to Backworth. Scrapping took place in 1966.
64 Far far away from its original home, plodding northwards from Tyneside (the NCB line to the staithes closed in 1969), is an ex. Port Talbot Railway saddle tank which went to Backworth Collieries Ltd from the GWR in 1934. Built by Hudswell Clarke of Leeds in 1901 (Works number 555) it bore PTR No. 26; GWR 813; Backworth 12 and NCB No. 11 before finally going to the Severn Valley Railway in 1967. (November 1963)

65
66

54

65 Coal was mined at Ashington, five miles north-west of Blyth, about the middle of the last century and in 1866 a railway was built two miles westward to join the North Eastern main line near Pegswood. The Ashington Coal Co. had inaugurated passenger services in 1895 when the two and a half mile railway to Linton Colliery opened, not only for the miners but also for use by the general public. Arriving at the Ashington terminus is No. 40, built in 1954 (R. Stephenson & Hawthorn 7765), with a rake of vintage NER stock beckoned on by signals operated from Ashington No. 1 Loop Box.

66 No. 39, seen here approaching Ellington, was also built in 1954 by the same maker (Works No. 7764) and scrapped in 1970 while No. 40 went to the North Norfolk Railway. Both were fitted with electric headlights.

67 Extensions to the Ashington system in 1930 (to Woodhorn) and in 1956 (Woodhorn to Lynemouth) completed the circle and in all some fifteen route miles were operated by a large fleet of locomotives. The Ashington to Ellington road was crossed, south of Linton, by the railway where an inside cylinder side tank No. 31 (R. Stephenson & Hawthorn 7609 of 1950) nears journeys end on passenger duty. Now preserved in north Yorkshire.

68 The passenger stock was no less interesting than the blue liveried locomotives and No. 29, northbound from Ashington, has a Furness Railway coach bringing up the rear of its train. Passenger services, which from 1949 had been for NCB personnel only, ceased operating in 1966. With the closure of Linton and Longhirst collieries, in 1968 and 1969, this section of railway fell into disuse and by 1970 steam working had finished too. No. 29 (RS&H Works No. 7607 of 1950) was scrapped in 1972, and the locomotive it is about to pass was No. 53 (Hunslet 3196 of 1944, ex WD 75145), scrapped in 1969.

(January 1966)

69

70

69 Eight miles north-west of Swansea lies Pontardulais with a three mile line to Graig Merthyr Colliery. Until 1970 workmen's passenger trains run for each shift, used also to deliver newspapers to a farm en route! At the half way stage on Gopa Hill *Graig Merthyr* (Andrew Barclay 1073 of 1906) pauses with a mid-afternoon working. 1073 was cut up in 1973.

70 Another colliery line which provided workmen's services was that from Talywain, near Pontypool, to the isolated Blaenserchan pit high up the valley. Former main line vans fitted with seats and handbrakes took the miners up grades as steep as 1 in 23 to the pit head. *Illtyd*, an Andrew Barclay outside cylinder saddle tank, passes derelict workings on the way to Blaenserchan with empties and a stores van. The line was lifted in 1970 but the loco remained at Talywain depot for shunting the Landsale yard which closed in 1974. *Illtyd* was built in 1952 (Works No. 2331). (May 1967)

71 By the end of the eighteenth century Merthyr Tydfil, at the head of the Taff Valley, was the centre of the South Wales iron industry. The nine mile Penydarren tramroad followed the river down to Abercynon, where it made connection with the Glamorganshire Canal, until closure in 1880. Treading the footsteps of Trevithick's engine is No. 1, an Andrew Barclay side tank (Works No. 2340 built 1953), returning to Merthyr Vale Colliery, Aberfan, from the exchange sidings of the former Taff Vale Railway. In the foreground can be seen quite clearly part of the trackbed of the Penydarren tramroad. (October 1968)

72 Propelling empty waggons towards Aberfan is Peckett No. 2061 (built 1945 for Slough Estates Ltd) one of a class of three locomotives known as OX3 with 16 in. × 24 in. outside cylinders. (November 1969)

73

74

73 In the next valley westwards, at the system centred on Mountain Ash, seven steam locomotives were still present in the mid 'seventies. Interconnected by rail links are Penrhiwceiber Colliery, Deep Duffryn Colliery and Abercwmboi Phurnacite plant near Aberaman. Shot from the window of a passing train approaching Cardiff Road station, Mountain Ash, on a line since taken over by the NCB, *Sir Gomer* seems to have fallen out with the permanent way. Peckett No. 1859 built 1932, formerly belonging to Powell Duffryn Ltd, is a class OX1 with 16 in. × 24 in. cylinders. (September 1962)

74 Both of these locomotives on shed at Mountain Ash, had a common ancestry in Messrs Fox, Walker & Co. of Bristol, taken over by Peckett & Sons in 1880. Edwin Walker then joined the ailing Avonside Engine Co. Ltd which closed down, but Walker formed a new company with the same name for building mainly industrial type locomotives. Avonsides finally shut down in 1934 while the Peckett firm lasted until 1959. Dumped, awaiting dismantling, is *The Earl* (Peckett 1203 of 1910, class B2) with 14 in. × 20 in. cylinders. Very much alive *Sir John* also a 14 in. × 20 in. engine put aside for possible preservation in 1974 (Avonside No. 1680 of 1914). *The Earl* was scrapped in 1973. (October 1968)

75 Contrasting styles in Avonsides wave a steamy greeting to one another across the Afon Cynon at Deep Duffryn Colliery. *Sir John* a late nineteenth century design, with a chimney which owes more to NCB than Bristol, looks somewhat puny against the beefy 16 in. × 24 in. cylinder *Lord Camrose* (Avonside No. 2008 of 1930) whose flat sided saddle tanks, Barclay style, were a feature of post World War I Avonsides. Both were originally owned by the Powell Duffryn Steam Coal Co. and appropriately dressed for Mountain Ash in coats of green. (November 1969)

76

76 Scotland, the home of Andrew Barclay, naturally saw more of that firm's products on industrial railways than those of other makers. Five 18 in. × 26 in. inside cylinder six-coupled side tanks were supplied to the Wemyss Private Railway during the 1930s for working from collieries in south Fifeshire to the docks at Methil on the Firth of Forth. No. 19 (Works No. 2067 of 1939) charges away from the docks towards Denbeath Washery while No. 17 (Works No. 2017 of 1935) idly doodles across the sky.

77 During the nineteenth century the owner of the Wemyss Estate, R. G. E. Wemyss, built his own railway (the Wemyss & Buckhaven Railway) which by 1887 reached Methil. Two years later the docks and the W&B Rly were bought by the North British Railway. Empties heading westwards towards East Wemyss behind No. 18 (Andrew Barclay 2048 of 1938), near Buckhaven, capture a main line atmosphere.

78 As the Wemyss Private Railway, built 1899, carried goods other than coal, and furthermore was not owned by the coal company, it was not nationalized in 1947 when the collieries and shunting locomotives became part of the NCB. The five brown liveried Barclays together with the system's brake vans stayed independent and worked the traffic between the pits, docks and washery for the NCB until gradual closures meant the end of yet another fine railway in 1970. Idyllic scenes such as this with No. 18 threading tall timbers near Buckhaven are gone except on film. No's 18 and 19 were scrapped in 1970, but No. 17 lingers on in a scrap merchant's yard and may yet be preserved.

(May 1966)

79 For over one hundred years the Doon Valley in Ayrshire has resounded to the forceful comings and goings of Andrew Barclay pugs around the collieries. The coalfield was first tapped near Patna in 1840. Ironstone was discovered incidentally and an ironworks was set up at Waterside in 1848. Twenty years later the first of a sequence of sturdy Barclays arrived, the successors of which are still at work at the two remaining collieries. At Dunaskin washery a former ironworks survivor with dumb buffers, No. 19 (Barclay 1614 of 1918), a four wheeler with 16 in. × 24 in. cylinders, quietly busies itself while on the far right, is No. 22, an 18 in. × 24 in. six wheel Barclay side tank (Works No. 1785 of 1923) which was scrapped in 1969.

80 By 1868 the first of many collieries near Pennyvenie had been sunk and the system extended. Two post-NCB Barclays at Pennyvenie obliterate the surrounding hills in swashbuckling style. No. 21 a 16 in. saddle tank (Works No. 2284 of 1949) vies with No. 24 a six wheel side tank with 18 in. cylinders (Works No. 2335 of 1953). The hideous chimney is a Giesl Ejector.

81 Waterside up to Pennyvenie is roughly four miles of hard slogging for which the 18 in. cylinder engines were more suitable than the four wheelers. Taking it casually down the last stretch from Minnivey to the washery is another link with the ironwork's days, No. 17, yet again from Andrew Barclay (1338 of 1913).

82 A highly practical feature of the Waterside system was the provision of coal tenders, an open ended waggon, for each of the tank locomotives enabling them to carry out a complete shift without recourse to the coal stocks. Putting their backs into it at Pennyvenie are the Giesl chimnied No. 24 (formerly No. 8) and No. 10 (erstwhile No. 1), Andrew Barclay 2244 of 1947, a similar machine to No. 21. Black is the standard livery. (May 1966)

83 Haig Colliery with workings under the sea, sits on the cliff top south of Whitehaven and its coal is washed at Ladysmith Preparation Plant a mile and a half to the south. Finished coal from Ladysmith used to be worked back over a steeply graded line, past Marchon Products at Kells, through Haig yard to the top of the 'Waggon Brake' and so down to the harbour. A tough job called for tough machines; 18 in. Austerity *Golborne* and 18 in. outside cylinder *Monaville* (R. Stephenson & Hawthorn 7176 of 1944 and 7606 of 1949 respectively) at Ladysmith. Both were scrapped in 1968. Worse still road transport took over in 1975.

84 Winding ceased at William Pit in 1955 but the loco shed remained in use. One of its more esoteric residents was *Ingwell* a hybrid 'bitser' cannibalized from scrapped locomotives at Lowca in 1962. Ostensibly it was an inside cylinder four-wheel Peckett saddle tank of class Y but the tank and chimney were from an Austerity! It is here unloading waste while beachcombers below search for bits of coal. On the far side of Whitehaven harbour may be discerned the Howgill Incline and the 1840 Wellington Pit 'candlestick' chimney. This odd little engine was scrapped in 1967.

85 R. Stephenson & Hawthorn 7049 of 1942 (formerly Workington Iron & Steel Co. No. 69), is seen sneaking around two vessels belonging to Marchon Products Ltd in Whitehaven's inner harbour.

86 By 1740 Whitehaven had become an important port and early wooden waggonways are recorded about this time. Only one colliery now remains open to testify to a once extensive industry. Waggons which have come down the Howgill Incline (closed in 1972) from Haig Colliery are here propelled away by Stephenson & Hawthorn 7049, broken up in 1973.   (June 1966)

85

86

87 Eight miles west of Manchester the headquarters and workshops of the former Manchester Collieries system at Walkden could always be relied on to provide some exotic types. Walkden's own speciality was the ex North Staffordshire 0-6-2 tanks. A Hunslet Austerity, *Repulse* (Hunslet 3698 of 1950) is shown coming up from Ellenbrook ex LNWR, sidings, towards Walkden yard, with Mosley Common Colliery away to the right.

88 A closer look at *Repulse* whence its chimney is revealed as a Giesl Ejector. About fifty NCB locomotives were so disfigured, including a few of Walkden's Austerities. The thirteen route-miles of the layout, included seven connections with main lines, giving two connections to power stations and two outlets on the Bridgewater Canal. Astley Green was the last operating colliery, which closed in 1970 together with the last remnants of the line. However the large workshops remained open for major repairs of locomotives some of which made their way here from South Wales.

89 As well as maintaining locomotives to work the system to Mosley Common Colliery, Brackley Colliery, Ashton Fields Colliery and Sandhole Colliery, Walkden yard was the dumping ground of locomotives awaiting works attention. Many of them were beyond repair and were cut up there. This trio awaiting final decimation are; ex Tyldesley Coal Co. Ltd *Jessie* an unusual four wheel side tank by Hunslet with 16 in. outside cylinders and Walschaerts valve gear (1557 of 1927); *Violet*, in danger of an indecent exposure offence, (Nasmyth Wilson 852 of 1908); and *Kenneth*, an ex North Staffordshire Railway 0-6-2 tank built at Stoke-on-Trent in 1921. They had all gone by March 1967.

(February 1966)

90 The largest concentration of steam power at any one location in the Yorkshire coalfield until the middle 'sixties, was at Manvers Main Colliery, a coal preparation and by-products complex near Wath-on-Dearne. A Yorkshire Engine Co. Ltd saddle tank, numbered 11 in the fleet, and built at Sheffield in 1922 (Works No. 1823) for the Wath Main Colliery Ltd sits inside the shed. It was scrapped in 1970.

91 Outside the loco shed at Manvers Main are – reading from the left – No. 50 a 200 h.p. vertical boiler Sentinel (9552 of 1953); *Wilf* a pre-NCB Manvers Main Collieries Ltd 16 in. × 22 in. Peckett X2 class (1891 of 1940); No. 51 (Hunslet 3834 of 1955); No. 48 (Hunslet 3685 of 1948); No. 49 *Ted* (Hunslet 3701 of 1950); No. 63 late BR 68067 and ex WD 71474 (Hudswell Clarke 1792 of 1944) and No. 65 (Hunslett 3889 of 1964). 65 was the penultimate standard gauge steam locomotive built in this country and was fitted with Hunslet underfeed stoker and gas producer system, as also was No. 63. Of the seven locomotives seen here only No. 65 remains, though still unemployed. (April 1969)

92 Walton Colliery, on the Wakefield–Doncaster line of the former West Riding and Grimsby Railway, provides a stirring sight as No. 34, a 15 in. × 22 in. outside cylinder saddle tank formerly *Sharlston No. 4* (Hudswell Clarke 1501 of 1923) blows its top, aided and abetted by sister loco No. 37 (Hudswell Clarke 1826 of 1950) giving a welcome shove in the rear up to the Midland Railway exchange sidings. No. 34 was scrapped in 1967 and No. 37 in 1969. (January 1964)

93 Three new Yorkshire Power Stations, built in the 'sixties, alone consume about twenty million tons of coal per year, much of which is carried on BR 'Merry-go-Round' trains. At Prince of Wales Colliery, Pontefract, the last built of the Hudswell Clarke side tanks (Works number 1886 of 1955) red liveried S 120, formerly *Whitwood No. 8*, marshalls 'Merry-go-Round' waggons. S 120 was scrapped in 1972. (November 1971)

94 A common sight in the colliery yards of the North Yorkshire area was the six wheel 16 in. × 24 in. outside cylinder side tank type built by Hudswell Clarke. During the 1960s Hunslet underfeed stokers were fitted to most NCB locomotives in this locality for smokeless working. Someone here, on *Fryston No. 2* (Hudswell Clarke 1883 of 1955) has resorted to wielding the shovel again, for sophisticated equipment such as this often tends to become neglected in the rough and tumble of everyday service. Green liveried *Fryston No. 2* worked at Fryston Colliery, and along a two mile connection to Wheldale Colliery, Castleford, (where coal washing facilities were shared) until 1972 when it was put to the torch.

95 Coal dug at Savile Colliery, near Methley Junction on the Sheffield to Leeds main line, goes out on the Aire & Calder Navigation. The locomotive striding away from the spoil tip is from Hunslet (works number 1956 of 1939). S 111 *Airedale No. 2* is a standard 16 in. × 22 in. cylinder saddle tank fitted with underfeed stoker. (September 1971)

96 Primrose Hill, where a steeply graded line ran down from the colliery about a mile and a half to staithes on the Aire & Calder Navigation just downstream of Savile basin, was closed in 1970. Empties returning to the colliery cling tight to a 16 in. Hunslet, S 117 *Astley* (Works No. 3509 of 1947), as they cross a road hard by Bowers Row disposal point. Bowers Row now uses the ex Primrose Hill staithes. (March 1969)

95

96

King Coal the Second

After World War II, many social and political changes took place which in no small way affected certain industrial railway systems. The Coal Industry Nationalization Act brought into being the National Coal Board, which from 1 January 1947 acquired and operated not only the collieries but also their brickworks, coking plants and railways. In one fell swoop over 950 collieries and more than 1500 steam locomotives became blanketed under the initials NCB.

With increasing modernization of machinery coal production began to rise, while the number of active pits continued to decline. Some indication of the extent of the industry during the last hundred years may be judged by the fact that while in 1880 there were 4231 collieries in Britain, this number had fallen to 3100 by the beginning of the First World War when the world record output of 287 million tons was achieved, in 1913. Of this total 87 million tons was exported, much of it from the South Wales coalfield where the only high grade anthracite in the country is won. At this time practically all the world's steamships were coal fired, but by the beginning of the Second World War the total had dropped by half. While this had caused a set back to the industry, the opening of new mines in Europe and the Far East in the 'twenties reduced even further the demand from our shores and was reflected in the cut back to 1400 collieries by 1926. Shortly before the industry was nationalized, production had fallen to 175 million tons, but rose again to 224 million by 1957. A programme of rationalization has left a mere 260 collieries operating in the early 'seventies – some 4000 less than a century ago – whose output is around 120 million tons, comparing favourably with the 147 million ton figure for 1880.

Not all coal, however, is won below the surface, nor is it all sold in its natural state. Where coal seams are to be found close to the surface the mineral is quarried in what are termed opencast sites where excavating is carried out by civil engineering contractors. The NCB Opencast Executive was set up in 1952 to control the sites formerly under the aegis of the Ministry of Fuel and Power. Where railways are employed, the locomotives are supplied either by the operating contractor or by the NCBOE. To the layman the most spectacular activity of the NCB is the coke ovens (from 1963 administered by a separate Coal Products Division) which metamorphose coal, in fiery furnaces, to produce smokeless fuel. Locomotives are used for shunting, transfer work, and on the quenching cars though the latter duty is normally the province of electric rather than steam locos.

As may be expected, some degree of standardization was bound to creep in to such a large organization, though in all areas 'off the peg' locomotives were still purchased over the next seventeen years. The locomotive which became a common sight almost everywhere throughout the industry was the Hunslet Austerity 0-6-0ST, originally designed in 1942 for the Ministry of Supply. In 1945 the first one not to be supplied to the government went to the Manchester Collieries Ltd and in the following year several ex-WD surplus examples were to be found at the Durham pits. Seemingly, the NCB were well satisfied with this class of locomotive, for they purchased more batches from the WD and ordered further construction, from 1948, which eventually totalled 77 machines. Others were purchased from British Railways and Port of London Authority until half the class, of which 484 had been built, saw service in the collieries. To the NCB goes the dubious honour of commissioning, in 1964, the last standard gauge steam locomotive to be built in this country – a Hunslet Austerity, in Hunslet's Centenary year.

Steam ended where it had begun – in industry.

98

99

97 Opencast mining is carried out by contractors some of whom employ their own locomotives to convey coal to the washeries and screens. Wm. Pepper & Co Ltd operated several sites between Sheffield and Wakefield, including Bowers Row Disposal Point six miles south-east of Leeds, where an Austerity class 0-6-0ST shunts near the screens. R. Stephenson & Hawthorn Ltd built ninety two locomotives of this design. Works number 7164 of 1944, originally WD 71510, had a peripatetic career among opencast sites before being scrapped in 1969.

(March 1969)

98 No. 47445, built in 1927 by Hunslet Engine Co. Ltd of Leeds as LMS 16528 (works number 1529), deposits a waggon on the staith for bottom unloading while the river Calder winds towards Wakefield in the distance. In 1970 diesels took over and 47445 went away to Derby for preservation.

99 The last steam locomotive to work British Oak Disposal Point, Crigglestone, four miles south-west of Wakefield, was No. 47445, purchased from BR in 1966, an ex LMS Fowler design, 18 in. × 26 in. cylindered side tank, to which Peppers applied a slightly unorthodox livery. The boiler and cab remained black but the side tanks and bunker were painted bright orange; red frame and coupling rods and a blue sandbox completed the ensemble.

(April 1969)

100

101

100 The situation at Staveley Works whereby ex LMS locomotives of BR were hired to do shunting had a parallel at Williamthorpe Colliery, also in Derbyshire but some five miles further south. Here the locomotives were the descendents of the Midland class 1 tanks at Staveley being designed by Henry Fowler in 1924. Westhouses' BR depot supplied two locomotives at a time to be driven by NCB crews on the coal hauls to North Wingfield. No. 47289 (North British Loco. Co. Ltd. 23130 of 1924) and No. 47629 (Wm. Beardmore 377 of 1928) appear to be taking on water simultaneously through one-inch garden hoses!

101 With 47629 piloting the same pair lead off from Williamthorpe into the autumn twilight. Both 47289 and 47629 went away for scrap in October 1967.

(September 1967)

102 This 'W6' class Peckett (1921 of 1936), No. 2 in the books of Derbyshire Coalite Co. Ltd at Bolsover and the smokeless fuel plant belonging to the Bolsover Collieries Ltd were not nationalized when the NCB took over the adjacent colliery in 1947. No. 2 lasted until 1969.

(May 1964)

103 Hudswell Clarke of the Jack Lane Works, Leeds, built their first locomotives in 1861 and for over one hundred years steam locomotive production continued until September 1961 when the last two, four-wheeled saddle tanks, for the NCB were outshopped. In 1906, Works No. 750, then named *Waleswood* for the Waleswood Colliery was built. Almost sixty years later it was still in the same vicinity, at Kiveton Park Colliery, eight miles out of Sheffield on the ex GCR Retford line. No. 750 was purchased for private preservation in 1972.

(May 1963)

104 Between Derby and Sheffield a branch line leaves the main line at Duffield and runs eight miles to Wirksworth, once a rich lead mining district dating back to Roman times. Middle Peak Quarries at Wirksworth were operated by Bowne & Shaw Ltd sending the limestone for use as flux in the iron industry. *Holwell No. 3* (Black, Hawthorn 266 of 1873) sets off for a nature ramble.

105 *Holwell No. 3* is not the only industrial locomotive to attain a working century but it must surely be the last. Built in 1873 by Black, Hawthorn & Co. Ltd, a company which operated from 1865 to 1896, in premises formerly occupied by an early Gateshead firm John Coulthard (established 1835), it came to Wirksworth in 1946 and is now a certainty for preservation. (June 1969)

106 Cement Works are normally situated where large deposits of chalk, or limestone are to be found and where there is adequate transport to bring in the coal necessary to heat the kilns. At Dunstable, in Bedfordshire, where the LNWR branch from Leighton Buzzard met a GNR branch from Hatfield, Houghton Regis cement works of the APCM donated their last two steam locomotives to the London Preservation Society. One of them was this Andrew Barclay (776 of 1896) named *Punch Hull*.

107 *Punch Hull* traverses the single line approximately half a mile long which connects the Works to the BR line, now running only as far as Luton. (May 1965)

106

107

108

109

108 North Kent was ideally situated for the manufacture of cement there being mile upon mile of chalk and an obliging Thames to bring in the coal and to take away the finished product. An early cement works was opened at Swanscombe in 1825, which from 1833 became known as White's Swanscombe Works, and a 3 ft 5½ in. gauge tramway was laid across the marshes to a jetty on the river. It was not until 1929 that standard gauge was adopted with five new locomotives from Hawthorn Leslie. Later came the two depicted here. In the distance No. 7 (R. Stephenson & Hawthorn 7405 of 1948) tightropes along a ledge while Hawthorn Leslie No. 3860 of 1935, masquerading as No. 3, hugs the bottom of the pit.   (December 1966)

109 As each train load arrived at the tipping points the locomotive unhooked and ran to the end of the line for coal and water while the waggons were emptied. No. 7, featured here again, was scrapped in 1972.
(January 1967)

110 After spending the rest of the year amid the chalk the last thing which No. 2 is dreaming of, on Christmas Eve 1966, is a White Christmas! The real No. 2 was Hawthorn Leslie No. 3716 of 1928 but No. 1 (Hawthorn Leslie 3715) swapped saddle tanks with it sometime during the sixties. No. 3715 is preserved at Ashford, No. 3716 was scrapped in 1972. Which one is at Bell Wharf while cement is loaded on to a coaster cannot be guaranteed.   (December 1966)

111 Some years before steam bowed out at Swanscombe in 1971 a game of 'swap the saddle tank' afflicted the 15 in. × 22 in. Hawthorn Leslies. In a cutting between two tunnels the 16 in. × 24 in. cylindered No. 7 propels empties towards the quarries while No. 3 starts another loaded train for the Works. No. 3 should be Hawthorn Leslie 3717 built 1928 but is more likely to be No. 6 (3860 of 1935) with the wrong saddle tanks!
(January 1967)

112 Kerr, Stuart 886 of 1905, *Premier*, the first of the Sittingbourne steamers.

Kentish Paper — Sittingbourne

Had it been possible to produce a book of this nature five hundred years ago it would have been necessary to use handmade paper, although in other parts of Europe a mechanical means of papermaking was already a reality. Towards the end of the fifteenth century a paper mill had been set up near Hertford, believed to have been the first in this country; and a century later the first mill is recorded in Kent, at Dartford. At that time best quality paper was made from linen rags pulped down with clean water, while inferior grades required flax, or hemp, cloth rags for production. It was owing to a shortage of suitable rags and the high import rate of superior continental paper that the establishment of mills in this country was such a slow process. One hundred mills were in operation by 1700, of which fourteen were situated in Kent, many employing foreign labour, and by the end of the century the total had increased to around four hundred. During the next ten years the industry underwent several changes for the better. Patents were granted for the pulping down of waste paper, straw, hay, thistles and wood, while china clay came into use as a whitening and smoothing agent. In France an endless-webb machine had been invented which produced paper up to five feet wide and 750 yards long. English patents were taken out for it in 1801, but workers fearing for their jobs put up stiff opposition, thus hampering a rapid adoption of its use.

Although Boulton & Watt steam driven machinery had begun to challenge the water mills in 1786, less than half employed steam forty years later. Apart from the basic ingredients required in the manufacture of paper, abundant supplies of pure clean water were essential, together with readily available coal, where steam was involved. North Kent was in a most favourable position because not only was transport by water, and the new railways, possible for the inward flow of raw materials and the outward despatch of the finished product, but there was also a proliferation of wells. Edward Lloyd set up a mill at Bow, East London, in 1861 and in 1877 founded the *Daily Chronicle Mill* at Sittingbourne, in which seven new machines were installed over twenty years. Here the largest machine then in existence, producing paper over ten feet wide, was in operation by 1884. Two miles north of Sittingbourne is Kemsley where a new mill was opened in 1925, bringing the total of machines for the two plants up to eighteen. Throughout these changes the name had remained the same but in 1948 Edward Lloyd Ltd became part of the Bowater group under the title of Bowaters Lloyd

Pulp and Paper Mills, which became Bowaters United Kingdom Paper Co. Ltd seven years later. Today, Kemsley Mill with its six machines produces untold miles of newsprint.

The Isle of Sheppey in the Thames estuary is separated from the mainland by a strait called the Swale, from which meanders Milton Creek. It was on Milton Creek that barges from Queenborough made connection with a horse-drawn narrow gauge railway, half a mile long, from the wharf to Sittingbourne. Just when this line was laid down is not certain, for many of Lloyd's records were destroyed by fire, but in 1913 a new dock on the Swale, capable of handling ocean-going vessels was commenced and the 2 ft 6 in. gauge railway was extended four miles to Ridham. When Kemsley Mill was built the railway was doubled from Ridham Dock to the new premises – a distance of $1\frac{1}{2}$ miles – where extensive sidings were developed. Both Kemsley and Ridham Dock were connected by standard gauge to the Sheerness branch of the main line, originally opened by the London Chatham & Dover Railway in 1860. Until 1936 when Lloyds purchased a Bagnall saddle tank appropriately named *Jubilee*, locomotives of the Southern Railway worked into the premises. Steam on the narrow gauge came in 1905 with the first of four 0-4-2 saddle tanks from Kerr, Stuart, the last of which was fitted, most unusually, with Hackworths valve gear. Before this latter arrived Kerr, Stuarts supplied an 0-6-2 side tank, in 1920, which set the pattern for the next two decades when four similar machines were built by Bagnall and a fifth was purchased from the Lodge Hill & Upnor Railway near Strood. This one, however was built by Manning Wardle of Leeds in 1915. There were also two fireless locomotives plus a small four-wheeler, which laboured under the name of *Rattler,* and the *pièce de résistance*: a single boiler, double engined, rigid frame side tank. All of these were from Bagnall's Works at Stafford, and the latter, which was one of seven similar locomotives originally designed for 2 ft 0 in. gauge lines in South Africa, was the last articulated locomotive to be built there – in 1953.

Rattler had a short life amid the pulp stacks. It was found to be too small for the heavy demands of the railway and was scrapped in 1950, having been purchased second-hand in 1942. Similarly *Monarch,* the big Bagnall, did not last until the system closed in 1969 though it was the youngest of the fleet and outlived by the original 1905 Kerr, Stuart. The apparent weakness of this locomotive was its marine-type boiler which was more costly to maintain than the orthodox firetube pattern and took an inordinately long time to raise steam. Perhaps its new owners, since 1966 the Welshpool & Llanfair Light Railway, will have more time on their side!

On the standard gauge there were but three locomotives during the steam era. *Jubilee* has already been mentioned and also the fact that main line engines were sometimes used. In latter years these were normally the ex-SECR Wainwright class P, 0-6-0 tanks, though it was not unknown for a 'Terrier' to participate. No. 31178, built at Ashford in 1910 as a passenger locomotive, had been loaned from BR on a number of occasions in time of need and when it was withdrawn from service it was bought by Bowaters, in 1958 and named *Pioneer II*. Its predecessor of the same name had been a Hunslet of 1867, rebuilt by Hudswell Clarke in 1906 and which came to Kent in 1942. One can imagine that on account of its age it was used mainly in a standby capacity for it lasted but eleven years before its ultimate withdrawal. The fate of the other two locomotives was sealed in 1968 when two redundant BR diesels were acquired. Fortunately both steamers have been preserved. Unfortunately, diesels did not save the narrow gauge.

Apart from the normal industrial duties of moving trains of timber, wood pulp, and china clay, on sideless high-ended bogie waggons or four-wheeled tipping trucks, totalling over four hundred items, there were the workmen's passenger trains which performed all round the clock services. Originally, these were formed of open 'coaches', soon to be replaced by seven covered carriages. In 1957 these were withdrawn and five new coaches built from steel-ended pulp waggons, which lasted until the service finally ceased in 1968. The previous year saw the introduction of specially built tank waggons transporting china clay slurry on BR from Cornwall to Sittingbourne; and incoming pulp at Ridham Dock was collected by road transport during 1968. This left the railway to deal only with stores, heavy equipment, and waste, until in October 1969 it finally succumbed. However, all was not lost for the directors of Bowaters had already become preservation minded and arrangements had been made to lease almost two miles of railway outside the immediate vicinity of the Sittingbourne and the Kemsley mills. Seven of the steam locomotives, five passenger coaches and some waggons were made available to the Sittingbourne & Kemsley Light Railway operated by the Locomotive Club of Great Britain. Excluded, was the locomotive Works at Kemsley. opened in 1954, but the engine shed from Sittingbourne is to be re-erected at the new terminus near Milton Creek, where a museum is also in the course of being set up. New passenger platforms, with refreshment facilities, are provided for an ever increasing number of passengers and while the Kemsley marshes may not be the ideal tourist attraction the lure of steam will not be denied. What is more one has the delight of travelling on a genuine industrial railway.

113 Two of the Bagnall built 0-6-2 tanks on the fourteen mile track of Bowater's narrow gauge railway at the Ridham end of the line. *Triumph* (Works No. 2511 of 1934) sets its train back into the sidings watched approvingly by sister *Superb* (Works No. 2624 of 1940). Both locomotives now operate under the LCGB Sittingbourne & Kemsley banner. In the right background stands the Kings Ferry bridge which carries rail and road over the Swale across to the Isle of Sheppey.

114 *Superb* on a passenger working eases away from Ridham dock with Sittingbourne in mind. The bogie coaches, which were rebuilt from pulp waggons, could accommodate twenty persons on wooden tramcar-type benches.

115 The comprehensively equipped heavy repair shops were opened at Kemsley in 1954, where two of the system's 0-6-2 tanks are in for attention. *Superior* (right), without a dome or spark arrester, was the first of that wheel arrangement to be delivered to Sittingbourne, in 1920, from Kerr, Stuart & Co Ltd (Works No. 4034) but the last from that particular Staffordshire firm. W. G. Bagnall Ltd built *Alpha* (2472 of 1932) developed from the Kerr, Stuart design, with the same 10 in. × 15 in. cylinders. Both are still extant; *Alpha* on home territory and *Superior* at Whipsnade Zoo.

(September 1969)

116 Of the fourteen narrow gauge locos operated by Bowater Lloyd one only was not built in Staffordshire. *Chevallier* was a Leeds product by Manning Wardle (1877 of 1915). The Kerr, Stuart *Superior* is in the centre and on the right *Conqueror*, a larger Bagnall (2192 of 1922) with 13 in. × 18 in. cylinders, completes a splendid trio at Kemsley Mills shed. (July 1961)

117 Across the wild expanse of marshland and the prospect of Milton bank ahead a train loaded with pulp beats a relentless tattoo on the line between Kemsley and Sittingbourne. *Melior*, one of the four 0-4-2 saddle tanks provided by Kerr, Stuart (Works No. 4219, built 1924) still belongs to Bowaters though leased to the Sittingbourne & Kemsley Light Railway. (October 1969)

118 Bowater's staff took great pride in their railway as exemplified by the spruce appearance of the green liveried locomotives. Here at Sittingbourne shed *Melior*, the Hackworth valve gear engine, receives expert attention while *Superb* relaxes off duty. (July 1961)

119 When Edward Lloyd set up his new mill at Sittingbourne in 1877 the pulp arrived alongside Milton Creek wharf by barge from Queenborough, on the Isle of Sheppey, where it had been off-loaded from Lloyd's own steamers. In 1906 a deep water dock was built at Ridham. On the eve of closure, by mountains of waste at Milton Creek, *Melior* reflects sadly over the forty-five happy years spent on the system. (October 1969)

118
119

120 Some seven miles upstream from Swanscombe's Bell Wharf, near the Erith marshes at Belvedere, another jetty was for nearly seventy years under the constant tread of 3 ft 6½ in. gauge locomotives. The works of Callenders Cable Construction Co. Ltd (British Insulated Callenders Cables Ltd since 1945) employed steam traction from 1900 when a small Bagnall was put into service for conveying materials around the Works and up to the jetty. Six steam locomotives were owned by BICC, the last being two green, four wheel Bagnalls *Woto* (2133 of 1924) and *Sir Tom* (2135 of 1925).

121 Castle Engine Works at Stafford was founded by W. G. Bagnall in 1875. In the following year their first railway locomotive was built, a standard gauge tank engine, which oddly enough did not set the pattern for the future because the majority of their products right down to the last steamer, built in 1957, were narrow gauge. Between 1892 and 1953 the circular marine-type firebox, saddle tank locomotive was a standard design.

Woto and *Sir Tom* had 7 in. × 12 in. cylinders, Walschaerts valve gear and were oil-fired. The large tank on the left side of the cab contains the fuel. Both locomotives are privately preserved.   (August 1967)

120
121

122 *Fire Queen*, built by A. Horlock & Co. Northfleet in 1848, incarcerated from 1886 to 1969 at Llanberis.

Snowdonia Slate

Narrow Gauge and North Wales are synonymous terms, especially so over the last two decades since the railway preservation movement was born. The Snowdon range of mountains, now a National Park, is coveted by tourists and those not energetically disposed may ride from Llanberis village to the summit on the only rack railway in Great Britain. Across the road from the Snowdon Mountain Railway station, rising over 2200 feet from the shore of Llyn Peris is Elidir Fach, a mountain of slate; part of the Cambrian slate belt, some 2500 feet thick, extending over twelve miles from Bethesda to Penygroes. As with coal, the Romans quarried slate from the outcrops as early as the third century but it was not until late in the eighteenth century that the industry was organized and developed in a big way.

Richard Pennant (later Lord Penrhyn) bought up the many quarrying partnerships on the Penrhyn estate and built roads from Glan Ogwen (now Bethesda) to a new harbour, opened in 1770, just east of Bangor. Slate from the quarries was transported by horse to the river Ogwen, and thence by boat to Port Penrhyn. In 1801 a nominal 2 ft 0 in. gauge railway, some six miles long close by the river, was built, with oval rails, from Penrhyn quarries to the port. Three inclined planes were a feature of the railway which was worked by horse traction. Much of the slate quarried was shipped for export, while for the home market a branch from the Chester to Holyhead main line was built to the port in 1852. Steam was introduced in 1876 following the re-alignment of the narrow gauge railway alongside the river Cegin, making a route of fairly even gradients. It is possible that one of the first locomotives to work on the line was a Lewin, but De Winton horizontal boilered locomotives, built locally at Caernarvon, bore the brunt of the early work. With the advent of more powerful, Hunslet built, locomotives the 'main line' was relaid with chaired rails, in 1883, circumscribing a loop at the end of the quay and crossing, in movable sections, the standard gauge tracks. Quarry workings bit into the mountainside while steam-worked tramways ran along a series of ledges, each about seventy feet high.

Returning to Llanberis, four miles south-west of Bethesda, the Dinorwic quarries had many features in common with their rival. It was the Assheton Smith family who developed Dinorwic in a fashion similar to the Penrhyn pattern. Slate had been carried by boat along Llyn Padarn, the larger of the two Llanberis lakes, then transferred to horse transport and subsequent shipment out of Caernarvon. Rails were first laid in 1824 to Velinheli (on the Menai Strait south-west of Bangor) where a new harbour, Port Dinorwic, was constructed seven miles from the quarries. This horse drawn line was superseded in 1843 by a 4 ft 0 in. gauge railway, further to the south, on which steam traction commenced in 1849 with the legendary *Fire Queen* (now preserved at Penrhyn Castle) and *Jenny Lind*. However, this railway did not operate on the quay and the narrow gauge quarry waggons arriving on transporter trucks were lowered down an inclined plane to another 2 ft 0 in. gauge system which, like that at Penrhyn, crossed the standard gauge branch at the port. The 'Padarn Railway' with its three Hunslet side tanks ceased work in 1961 and, tragically, the Dinorwic quarries with a fifty mile rail system closed down in 1969. Penrhyn's 'main line' ended in 1962 yet steam lingered at the quarries until 1965.

While Penrhyn quarries remain in limited production, the extensive workings on Elidir stand as a monumental epitaph to a once flourishing industry.

123

124

125

126
127

123 Penrhyn quarries 1 ft 10¾ in. gauge railways spread themselves throughout fifty miles of galleries and workshops worked by a fleet of diminutive black liveried locomotives of multifarious ancestry. *Glyder*, an 0-4-0 well tank of Orenstein & Koppel design, was built by Andrew Barclay in 1931 (Works No. 1994). After withdrawal it was preserved, along with many another North Wales narrow gauge locomotive, on the far side of the Atlantic.

124 *Marchlyn* a neat Avonside (2067 of 1933), might almost be on the moon for all the bleakness of its surroundings. *Marchlyn* gravitated to the USA in 1966 from Penrhyn.

125 Unlike the main line of the Dinorwic Company the Penrhyn equivalent was laid to the same gauge as the quarry system. *Blanche* (Hunslet 589 of 1893) passes under the Chester to Holyhead main line with a train load of well-dressed slates four years before being sold to the Festiniog Railway in 1963.

126 The Dinorwic Slate Quarries Railway of 4 ft 0 in. gauge was more popularly known as the Padarn Railway over which the narrow gauge slate waggons were conveyed on Host waggons, four to each, between the transfer point at Llanberis and Port Dinorwic. Here *Amalthaea* (Hunslet 410 of 1886) stands at Gilfach Ddu. She was scrapped in 1963.

127 Twenty-two examples of Hunslets in six different classes, spanned the period from 1870 to 1932 when the last one was delivered to Dinorwic Quarries. Eighteen of these have been preserved, including four which now work on the Llanberis Lake Railway running for two miles along the trackbed of the former 'Padarn Railway'. Red-coated *Covertcoat* (Hunslet 679 of 1898), a Port class engine, is here seen working at 900 ft above sea level. (July 1959)

128 Fireless locomotives operated for several hours on one charge of high pressure steam. *Unique* a 2-4-0 with $18\frac{1}{2}$ in. × 18 in. cylinders worked on the Bowaters railway, and was Bagnall's first fireless design (Works No. 2216 of 1923).

129 In 1893 De Winton of Caernarvon built *Watkin* a vertical boiler, vertical cylinder 3 ft 0 in. gauge locomotive. This Kingston Minerals Ltd loco at Penmaenmawr is now preserved at Penrhyn Castle.

130 Stanton Ironworks operated nine Kilmarnock-built cranes. *Stanton No. 24* (Barclay 1875 of 1925) is pictured at Riddings Foundry since when it has been preserved by the Midland Railway Co.

131 The more modern version of the vertical boilered locomotive was introduced by the Sentinel Steam Wagon & Carriage Co. Ltd of Shrewsbury in the early 1920s. A high pressure water tube boiler was situated in the cab while the bonnet housed four $6\frac{3}{4}$ in. × 9 in. cylinders with reduction gearing to the drive. *Joyce* is a 200 h.p. example (Works No. 7109 of 1927) formerly at Waddon Marsh gasworks, Croydon. Bressingham Hall Steam Museum is her present address.

132 Bowater's standard gauge *Jubilee* a typical Bagnall 12 in. × 18 in. saddle tank delivered to Edward Lloyd Ltd in 1936 (Works No. 2542). The 'greenhouse' cab was a common feature of this Kentish system. *Jubilee* found shelter with a Cambridgeshire collection in 1971.

133 *Pioneer II* designed by H. Wainwright for the South Eastern & Chatham Railway in 1909 as class P. 178 was built at Ashford in 1910 and withdrawn as BR 31178 in 1958. After working for Bowaters it was purchased by the Bluebell Railway in 1969.

133

134 This main line locomotive was one of a select few hired out to industry; in this case at Staveley Ironworks. BR 41533 was built at Derby in 1921 to the design of R. M. Deeley with 15 in. × 22 in. cylinders. It featured Walschaerts valve gear and a very un-Midland chimney. No. 41533 was scrapped in 1967.

134

135 Waddon Marsh Gasworks, Croydon, was host to *Moss Bay* a 15 in. × 20 in. cylinder saddle tank by Kerr, Stuart (4127 of 1920) a class which took its name from the Moss Bay Hematite Iron & Steel Co. who ordered the prototype in 1900. This 1920 example can be seen at Shugborough Hall Museum in Staffordshire.

136 This 0-6-2 tank was built as No. 28 by the Taff Vale Railway in 1897 at Cardiff (Works No. 306). After serving with the GWR, it was sold to the Longmoor Military Railway then in 1948 resold to the NCB at South Hetton as No. 67. Retired in 1960 it was sent back to South Wales for preservation at Caerphilly.

137 Beckton gasworks No. 1 dates from 1870 when it was built by Neilson & Co. of Glasgow (Works No. 1561). Observe the unusual outside Stephenson link motion. Penrhyn Castle is now the abode of this 10 in. × 18 in. well tank rarity which retired in 1962.

135

137 136

Appreciation

Mesmerized by the rhythm of wheels tapping on rail joints, the regular flick of poles, accompanied by the rise and fall of telegraph wires, the wisps of steam readily condensing in the cold air outside the warmth and cosy comfort of my compartment, I remember vividly how, suddenly, the sound of heavy industry jerked me back to reality. I swung round just in time to be briefly confronted by the impressive dominance of a steel works with several steam engines fussing about the feet of fiery furnaces. Immediately I was plunged into the darkness of a tunnel which effectively imprinted the scene on my senses – black, brown, red and white; metal, rust, spitting sparks and steam, movement and noise. An impressive introduction to industrial railways to which I was slow to respond. Seven years elapsed before I actually set foot in Corby.

This had been a bonus trip to Nottingham early in my days of railway exploration. Normally I could travel only as far as free time and grant allowed, which meant the northern environs of London, with a sketch book. Then I acquired, what at the time I misguidedly believed to be a corruptive influence, a camera. Initially I used it simply as a recording appendage to my art work, but it soon gained my respect and stood as an independent medium.

In time I became less shackled and was able to travel farther afield with British Railways as my quarry. However, after a few years of simply stumbling across various industrial lines, they came to take a rightful place in my esteem as part of a complete network, offering distinct variety and independence.

One consistent factor amidst all this diversity has been the welcome and help I have received from staff of the various undertakings. Frequently I have found myself invited to the shelter and warmth of a footplate or to share a life saving can of tea in a hut or lobby. Occasionally I would be offered something more substantial in a canteen or club, or proffered something less tangible like interest and information. All this and more have combined to make these pictures possible and of course enjoyable in the making.

These few pages linked by a personal favourite, the unpretentious, workmanlike 'Barclay', are my inadequate tribute to these men.

I extend my thanks specifically to Nigel Willoughby and Horace Gamble. Nigel, for his companionship and constructive criticism and to whom much credit for what you see in these pages is due. Horace, for his willing response when the book was first mooted and his dedication thereafter. It has been a pleasure to work with him and, like myself, I am sure you find his work both informative and a pleasure to read.

CTG.

138 The crew of 2217, built in 1947, relax on a warm September afternoon in 1969 at the Kilnhurst plant of Yorkshire Tar Distillers Ltd.

139 Three 'gents' at Ladysmith, Whitehaven in 1965.

140 Beside the main line near Lochgelly 2261 of 1949 gently propels waggons for a count before returning to Nellie Colliery in June 1965.

141 Before retiring to shed on a May evening in 1967, *Toto No. 6* Works number 1619 of 1919 (which contains parts and carries works plates from 1502 of 1917) re-arranges a few waggons at the end of the line on the edge of Blaenavon town.

Steam in Twilight

A valiant rearguard soldiers on
Now that the main line troops have fled.
Upholds the tattered flag of steam against the wind of change
That blows across the land of Stephenson.
How long, how long will they remain?
This faithful, rugged, battered band
Oozing through the muddy yards around the pits,
The factories, docks.
Pensioners from a golden age
Before the dark dread hordes of Diesel came
To oust them from their smoke-clad steamy chores,
Clanking, snorting,
Hauling monster loads of coke and coal
China clay or iron ore.
Where once Industry could command a regiment of saddle tanks,
Hunslet, Kitson, Hudswell Clarke,
Bred like tykes on Yorkshire soil;
Now in their stead the rumbling Ruston drones
Among the serried ranks of wooden trucks,
Buffeting over rickety tracks,
Clickety clacks towards the woeful shed
Within whose white-washed walls a Peckett waits
In patience, for a summary call to deputize.
So for a brief and glorious summer
Shouts to the sky with joy unpent and beating breath.
Then round the coal-black coal stacks stalks
Like Walkden's *Warspite, Warrior, Wasp,*
Now gone alas
To breaker's torch.
The fires keep dropping, one by one,
From Corby's Pen Green (pleasant land!)
To Seaham, Swanscombe, Mountain Ash.
Then blackbirds nest beneath a rusty frame,
By tarnished spokes and slidebar gear.
With brasswork dim and worksplates gone,
They silent stand in sleet and snow,
Or scorching summer sun
When gentle zephyrs waft the waving grass
Among their idle wheels.
By gasworks gate or cooling tower,
Yearning.
Yet warming steam may surge again,
Renew them with a lease of life
So precious, short.
Remember *Betty, Bursar, Barabel?*
Alas now gone
To molten grave.

H.A.G.

Index

Acton Lane 46
Armstrong Whitworth, Sir W. G., Ltd 44
Ashford 22, 81
Ashington 54, 55
Avonside Engine Co. Ltd 59, 89
Aberfan 57

Backworth 53
Bagnall, W. G., Ltd 22, 81, 83, 84, 86, 90
Barclay, Andrew, Sons & Co. Ltd 22, 23, 27, 31, 32, 34, 46, 57, 61, 63, 76, 89, 90, 92, 93, 94
Beardmore, W. 75
Beckton 91
Bethesda 87
Bessemer 10
Beyer Peacock & Co. Ltd 40, 42
Blaenau Ffestiniog 8
Blaenavon 94
Blaydon 45, 49
Black, Hawthorn & Co. Ltd 19, 76
Blenkinsop 11, 12
Blaenserchan 57
Bolsover 75
Bowaters 80, 81, 83, 90, 91
Bowers Row 70, 72
Buckhaven 61
Burntisland 36

Caledonian Railway 28
Cambois 53
Cardiff 36, 91
Castleford 70
Chatham 22
Coalbrookdale 8, 10, 11, 26
Corby 26–31, 92
Crigglestone 73
Croydon 90, 91

Darby, Abraham 26
Darlington 8, 10, 13
Derby 10, 34, 91
Derwenthaugh 49
De Winton & Co. 87, 90
Dinorwic 87, 89
District Railway 40, 41
Doxford and Sunderland Shipbuilding & Engineering Co. Ltd 24, 25
Dunaskin 63
Dunstable 76

Ellington 55
English Electric Co. Ltd 19
Esholt 39
Erith 86

Falmouth 22
Fire Queen 87
Fowler, J. 40
Fryston 70

Glasshoughton 49
Graig Merthyr 57
Great Central Railway 42, 43
Great Northern Railway 40, 41, 45
Great Western Railway 8, 40, 41, 42, 44

Hackworth, T. 12, 13, 84
Hawthorn Leslie, R. & W. & Co. Ltd 13, 16, 19, 24, 27, 28, 30, 31, 43, 49, 78
Hedley, W. 12, 13
Hetton 12, 17, 50
Head Wrightson & Co. Ltd 19
Horlock, A. 87
Howgill Incline 8, 64
Hudswell, Clarke & Co. Ltd 22, 27, 29, 36, 39, 42, 46, 53, 68, 70, 75
Hunslet Engine Co. Ltd 19, 26, 27, 28, 30, 31, 32, 42, 55, 67, 68, 70, 72, 73, 81, 89

Inverkeithing 22

Kemsley 80, 81, 83, 84
Kerr, Stuart & Co. Ltd 42, 44, 80, 81, 83, 84, 91
Killingworth 11, 12, 13
Kilnhurst 92
Kitson & Co. Ltd 28, 29, 31, 50

Ladysmith 64, 93
Lambton, 49, 50
Lewin, S. 15, 19, 20, 21
Lillie Bridge 42, 45
Linton 55
Liverpool & Manchester Rly 13
Llanberis 11, 87
Lloyd, E. 80
Locomotion 8, 13
London Chatham & Dover Rly 41, 81
Londonderry Railway 17, 18, 19
London & North Western Rly 10, 67
Losh, W. 10, 12

Manning Wardle & Co. Ltd 19, 27, 28, 31, 42, 81, 84
Manvers Main 68
Merthyr Vale 57
Methley 49, 70
Metropolitan Rly 40–43
Methil 61
Middleton Railway 11, 12, 48
Midland Railway 10, 26, 34, 41, 45
Mirfield 36
Mountain Ash 59
Murray, M. 12

Nasmyth Wilson & Co. Ltd 67
Neasden 42, 43, 45
Nellie Colliery 93
Newcastle 10, 13, 14, 28
Newport (Mon.) 32
Neilson & Co. 91
North British Loco Co. Ltd 41, 44, 75
North British Railway 22, 23
North Eastern Railway 10, 18, 19, 50, 53, 55
Norwood 49

Orenstein & Koppel, A. G. 89
Outram, B. 10, 11

Paddle Steamers 15, 18, 19
Par 22
Pearson, C. 40, 41
Penarth 36
Penydarren 10, 11, 57
Pennyvenie 63
Peckett & Sons Ltd 19, 24, 27, 36, 42, 43, 57, 59, 64, 68, 75
Penmaenmawr 90
Penrhyn 87, 89
Padarn Railway 11, 87
Pontefract 49, 68
Primrose Hill 70
Prince of Wales 68

Riddings 34, 90
Ridham 81, 83
Rocket 13, 14

Sanspariel 13
Savile 2, 70
Scunthorpe 32
Seaham 15–21
Sentinel Steam Carriage & Wagon Co. Ltd 30, 68, 90
Sharp, Stewart & Co. Ltd 42
Sittingbourne 80–84
South Eastern & Chatham Rly 91
Staveley 34, 35
Stella 46
Stephenson, G. 10–13, 46, 50, 53
Stephenson, R. 11, 13
Stephenson, Robert & Co. Ltd 8, 13, 40, 50
Stephenson, Robert & Hawthorns Ltd 16, 24, 27, 28, 31, 32, 46, 49, 53, 55, 64, 73, 78
Stoke-on-Trent 67
Stockton & Darlington Railroad 11, 13
Stuart Street 46
Swanscombe 78
Swindon 42, 44
Snowdon 87

Taff Vale Railway 36, 57, 91
Trevithick, R. 10, 11, 12

Vulcan Foundry Ltd 34, 49, 53

Walton 68
Walkden 67
Waterside 63
Wemyss Private Railway 61
Whitehaven 8, 12, 64
Widened Lines 40, 41, 44, 45
Williamthorpe 75
Wirksworth 76
Workington 32, 33
Wylam 10–13, 46

Yorkshire Engine Co. Ltd 27, 43, 68